PUSH THE RED BUTTON

PUSH THE RED BUTTON

WHEN TRAVEL IS AN ADVENTURE

Van Chesnutt

This book is collection of personal travel related experiences. Its purpose is to entertain and educate. I have tried to recreate events and locales to the best of my memory of them. In order to maintain the anonymity of some of the individuals mentioned, other than my wife and I, their names have been changed. In a few cases I have changed some identifying characteristics and details of physical properties and places. No other identification with actual persons, living or dead, is intended or should be inferred. Well, maybe the dead.

2019 Means To An End

Published in the United States of America by Means To An End, Inc.

ISBN 978-0-9995852-2-1
ISBN-13: 978-0999585221 (Means To An End)

eBook ISBN 978-0-9995852-1-4
Library of Congress Control Number: 2019901229

Dedication

This book is dedicated to my wife, Shirley. She and I have experienced most of the stories you will find in this book. Her love, humor and sense of adventure have brought much joy to my life.

Table of Contents

Preface

Push the Red Button is a book for people who like to travel, seasoned or just getting started, who see life and travel in particular as an adventure. It is a collection of amusing anecdotes, incidents, or just plain observations experienced over 30-plus years of travel.

Stories are grouped either by location—things that occurred in a particular country, or by a theme such as incidents related to things mechanical. They are in no specific time orientation, nor are they necessarily related except by country or theme.

I hope the descriptions and observations that follow will bring a smile to your face or an appreciation for the ordinary things that can make a moment extraordinary.

1. Curious

Curious things, incidents and unanticipated events happen when traveling. Events that are seemingly random, not necessarily related to anything at all. This chapter is a few of those.

An Intimidating Start

"And why are you coming to Canada?" asked the Canadian customs and immigration officer.

I had no idea. I didn't know what to say. I had no idea why we were coming to Canada.

I just stood there looking at him. All kinds of answers ran through my head. The first one was, "Because it made the airfare $4 cheaper." That might not be the best thing to say. It might be considered rather insulting.

I could tell him that my travel agent said we had time to squeeze it in. That wasn't the best answer either. I looked at my wife, the first Mrs. C. She apparently did not know why we were there either.

The officer, to his credit, seeing the deer-in-the-headlights look, offered, "Are you here on business or holiday?"

Being the quick thinker that I am, I thought, "Holiday, that's the British term for vacation. Yes, that's it!"

I said, "Yes, yes, we're on holiday. That's it."

He let us into the country regardless of our behavior, probably thinking that such stupid people would be of no great threat to Canada.

***

In the Beginning

Almost as far back as I can remember I have traveled. Growing up in Miami, I'd travel up to north Florida or south Georgia with my grandmother to see relatives and to spend part of the summer. As a child I'd follow our journey on the map. I didn't ask, "Are we there yet?" Instead I'd point to the map and say, "This is where we are".

As I grew older, and after my parents were divorced, I would fly from Miami up to Atlanta on Christmas Day to see my father. Traveling, going somewhere different, was what I did. It was an adventure, and I did not think it uncommon.

When I got married, my first wife and I would travel from Miami to New Jersey to visit her relatives. On occasion we ventured into New York City or up into New England. A bit later, when we could afford it, we decided to see the United States. There was an advertisement at the time that said, "See America first." We thought this was a good idea. Our first big trip where we would not see relatives was to the American west. We began in Vancouver, Canada.

***

Now, back to the question at Canadian customs. A friend had recommended a travel agent named Paul to help us. When we told him we wanted to see the western states, he told us that some airlines had fly-drives packages that we could take advantage of. Specifically, we could fly to a city, get a rental car, drive to another city then fly somewhere else from there. He did a lot of work to figure out an itinerary that would work for us at a reasonable price. Our plans included: Las Vegas, the Grand Canyon, San Francisco and Los Angeles.

We would fly home to Miami from LA. As he said, some of our transportation between destinations was by air and some by car.

A few days before we were to leave, Paul called us and said, "How about adding Vancouver, British Columbia to your trip? The air fare is based on your farthest destination and if you go Vancouver, you can save $4 per ticket and you get an extra city."

We said, "Sure. Why not? Four bucks is four bucks." As I said, telling the Customs officer that I was coming to Canada because it was four dollars cheaper did not seem like a good idea.

Easy Walk

Later in that same trip, we were driving through Utah and had the opportunity to visit Zion Canyon. Zion is gorgeous, by the way, and very different for someone from Florida. We had planned to stay the night in the Canyon Lodge, but when we arrived our room wasn't ready, so we decided drive on through the canyon for a while to kill some time. We stopped at a picnic area and we saw a sign that read, "Weeping Rock, easy walk—1/4 mile."

Hey, we could do this. So we started to walk. After not too long, we came upon something that might be Weeping Rock—the rock face of the canyon wall was damp. There was no signpost, so we kept going. We kept going and going and going and going. I finally turned to my wife and said, "If they think this is an easy walk, people are going to be in for a big surprise!" We went on a little farther and then decided to turn back; we had gone much farther than a quarter mile. When we got back to trail head, we inspected the sign to see where we had gone wrong. We discovered there were two signs. One read, "Canyon Ridge—5 miles, experienced hikers," and the other, right above it, "Weeping Rock." We might have taken the wrong trail, but to this day I still think we were on the *easy* walk.

Coincidently, when I told the current Mrs. C. about Weeping Rock, she told me she had experienced the same issue when she had visited Zion with her parents many years before.

Now, when anything supposedly easy in fact turns out to be difficult, we think, "Weeping Rock—easy walk."

CIGSMARBASIN

We never did stay at the Zion Canyon Lodge that evening because our room never got made up, so instead we drove on out of the park and stopped for the night at a little motel in Hurricane, Utah. As it turned out, it was a terrific motel; it had a super little restaurant for guests (and I presume locals too) above the office. Dinner was exceptional and my steak was so large it hung off the plate. The point in mentioning this motel however, is not the restaurant, but the bathroom in our room. After we checked in, I was exploring our room, checking things out as men so often do, when I noticed a bright red *Dymo* stick-on label on the top of the sink. It read "CIGSMARBASIN." What the hell was that supposed to mean? Every time I went to the sink I saw it and wondered. The next morning, I said to my wife, "What do you suppose this means?" She looked at it for a moment and *slowly* said, "CIGS MAR BASIN"—"Cigarettes mar the basin. Don't rest your cigarettes on the sink; they mar it if they burn on it." Obviously, if composite words had been a category on *Jeopardy*, I would have missed this one.

Buckets of Water

Whether or not it is true or not—I believed it to be at the time—Moab, Utah is one of the premier white-water rafting centers of the US. It should be; it is right on the Colorado River.

We were headed north on highway 161 through Moab one September morning when I saw a sign that read, "White Water River Rafting—Available."

I said to my wife, "Did you see that sign about river rafting? Let's check it out." She said okay, so I turned the car around to find out more.

Inside the office of the outfitter, I learned that there were indeed a couple of places available, and it was extremely well priced. They said that there were three boats that would be ready to go in about five minutes and that we'd be back around five in the afternoon.

We had to make our decision fast; it was "Let's go for it." We paid for our excursion and were pretty much ready to go.

We grabbed what we needed from the car, which wasn't much, climbed into one of the 4x4 vehicles towing a large river raft behind it, and were off on our adventure.

It wasn't long before we got to the river and helped slide the boats off the trailer into the Colorado. Our boatman, Randy, gave each of the four couples in our boat an army ammo can and said, "Put anything you don't want to get wet in here." After we'd all done this, he checked to make sure they were all properly sealed. We'd meet the 4x4s and trailers downstream later in the afternoon.

After Randy tied down the cooler that contained our lunch and some cold drinks, everyone climbed aboard, and Randy pushed our boat into the river. He sat in the middle with two very large oars. Two couples sat in the front and two in the back. It did not really matter much which was the front and which was the back, as it could and would change moment to moment.

One couple in the front of the raft I found interesting. Their names were something like David and Diane. What I found interesting was that they seemed to be a tad bit overdressed for river rafting, Diane in particular.

It wasn't long before we encountered our first set of rapids. It was exhilarating. Randy tried to keep one end of the boat pointed downstream with the oars, but the rapids bounced us around quite a bit and splashed this way and that. Everyone helped out with the bailing buckets. Diane did not get wet.

I thought getting wet was okay, as it was getting a bit warm; good thing we had hats. Throughout the morning and past noon, we had some smooth sections of the river and more sets of rapids, some rougher than others. Everyone seemed to be having a grand time and relished the cool water, but Diane did not get wet. In fact, she hardly had a hair out of place. How was this possible?

In the early afternoon, all the boats pulled up onto a shallow beach for lunch. We had all the fixings for some super sandwiches and some fruit and cookies.

One of the men from our boat asked if there were any fish in the river. You couldn't see any; the water was too muddy, but they were there. That said, if you put a piece of bread on the water next to the boat, you'd see a little mouth suck it away rather quickly.

Randy said we could go swimming if we so desired, but my initial thought was, "Isn't the water going to be a bit cold, particularly with this being water coming out of the mountains, off of snow?" The answer was, "Not so much." The air temperature had now passed from warm to hot. I went in the water and it felt good.

After lunch, with the boat packed, we set out on the river again. Randy told me I could float in the river, near the boat, as long as I had shoes on and kept my feet downstream. He said that when we approached any significant rapids, I should climb back in the boat, but for the smaller ones, I should be okay. Now this was fun!

We went through several sections of rapids, some small, some larger. Eventually, though, I was back in the boat full time. No matter what, Diane did not get wet.

We made an afternoon stop or two before sighting our destination down river in a wide calm spot.

Whether or not it is customary, a water fight broke out between the boats. Using the bailing buckets, everyone in all the boats was flinging water at each other. It was great fun. We were all kids again. Diane got wet. Diane got soaked. As it turns out, Diane was quite skilled at water flinging and she seemed to really get in to it. I guess she figured, "What the hell."

The preceding stories took place with my first wife, Barbara, before I moved to Seattle and remarried. I mention this so as not to cause confusion when I refer to Mrs. C. Going forward, Mrs. C. is Shirley.

No Pockets

On St. Martin, in the Caribbean, we had rented a house/villa for a few days from Green Cay Villas. The furnishings of the villa were light, airy and contemporary, with a beautiful view down the hill toward Orient Beach. The refrigerator was stocked with Coke, beer, champagne, wine, bread and eggs, all just to get you started. We were told that there were a couple of restaurants along the beach so that's where we headed to get some lunch.

Lunch consisted of pizza and Cokes under a thatched roof and watching the people on the beach. On Orient Beach people wear either very skimpy swimsuits or no suits at all—which was a big surprise to my wife. She had no idea. In fact, our first exposure to the no suits option was a man who went up to the bar where we were having lunch and said, "I hear you have good pizza. I'd like to order one."

How could he order pizza? How was he going to pay? He had no clothes and no pockets. No pockets for money or a credit card.

Nonetheless the bartender took the pizza order without a second thought. About five minutes later, the man's significant other arrived. She had on only a yellow bikini bottom. She also had a little yellow purse with, I presume, money in it.

Like I said, we also had pizza, but I had pockets.

Buffalos and the Gene Pool

On a visit to Yellowstone National Park in late September, we stayed in the town of West Yellowstone, just outside the west entrance to the park. Staying outside the park was necessary as most of the main lodges in the park were already closed for the season. In addition to the geological things to see, like geysers and canyons, we were hoping to see a great many of the indigenous animals such as buffalo, elk, bear, etc. We were not to be disappointed.

On one of our sojourns into Yellowstone we were headed back to our hotel along the park's west highway when we encountered a herd of buffalo on the road—a not uncommon occurrence. They, after all, own the place. Cars were stopped and people were taking pictures. No one seemed to be in any particular hurry, especially the buffalo. Then a woman got out of her car to get some better, up close pictures of the buffalo. Uh-oh, I thought. This might not end well. These are wild creatures and not necessarily friendly toward us humans and she was getting far too close to them. Seemingly all of a sudden, a clearing appeared in the herd and we, in our car, were able to get through and on to our destination.

We did not hear of anyone getting killed while we were there, but there have been numerous instances of people getting out of their cars and getting injured by buffalo. If you mess with buffalo, you could end up being gored or killed. If you are killed, you could win a Darwin Award. Darwin Awards recognize individuals who, by their own actions have removed themselves from the gene pool. You could also gain national fame for being arrested for harassing the buffalo. It has happened.

There's Been a Coup

We were staying in the Yasawa Island group northwest of the main Fijian island of Viti Levu in the South Pacific. We were there for a few days to take advantage of the fabulous snorkeling. Accommodations at the resort are individual *bures* set back a little ways from the beach and are quite spacious. A *bure* is a small structure, similar to a cabin that usually has a thatched roof. Ours was quite nice and it had a private outdoor shower.

One of more interesting things I remember about the island are the jumping crabs. They are black and blend in very well with the black rocks on parts of the shore. They literally jump from one rock to another. This can be a bit startling.

We had been told that generally the resort staff tends to leave you alone. In fact, if you really do not want to be disturbed, you leave a coconut with a plant sprouting out of it on the deck of your bure as a sort of "Do Not Disturb" sign. One afternoon, someone from the office brought us an envelope—even though our coconut was out. The envelope contained the following letter.

This is to inform you that there has been a non-military coup in Fiji and a new civilian government is being appointed today. We pass on this information not to alarm you, but just to keep you informed of events as they happen.

The events so far will in no way impact your holiday at Yasawa Island Resort. There are no interruptions to international flights at this stage.

We will keep you informed as we receive further news.

Hey, no worries. Other than the original note from the resort staff we received no further communication on the event. There was no television on the island, no Internet, and very little radio. We tried to get some news on the radio, but essentially there was nothing. We did learn that no one had been hurt or killed, but there was significant confusion in the capital of Suva on the southern part of main island of Viti Levu.

As for news, there was apparently not a great deal of information to be had.

When we went to leave, we flew from Yasawa to the main Fiji airport, Nadi International. Here we encountered some indications that things were not quite normal. We had arranged for a day room at a hotel near the airport, as our flight to the US was not until the late afternoon. We learned from the taxi driver that took us to our hotel that access to the airport was being restricted; he did not know why. Nonetheless, he told us that he would pick us up at the hotel a couple of hours before our flight and get us to the airport.

With the day room we could use the hotel's pool and have a nice lunch instead of hanging around at the airport. It was the South Pacific after all and it was hot and humid.

The taxi picked us up as planned and took us to the airport. There was limited access at the airport, but fortunately our driver apparently had a special pass of some sort. He dropped us off and we were able to get on our flight with no real complications and head back to the US.

Since the coup we experienced, they have had another one or two. To me, a foreigner, the reason for the coups seemed vague. It appears that there was substantial disagreement between the indigenous Fijians, the Indo-Fijians, i-Taukei nationalists, and the prime minister, who was of Indian descent. The Indians make up roughly 37 percent of the population. I never learned what the 'significant confusion' was in the capital, but I am grateful that the hotel staff ignored our do-not-disturb coconut to inform us of a coup.

The Pharaoh's Curse

We were on a tour in Egypt, staying in Cairo. Arrangements had been made for our group of seventeen to visit the Great Pyramid of Giza, also known as the Great Pyramid of Khufu. It was just after noon when we met our local host Ashraf in the hotel lobby. He introduced us to Layla, who would be our guide, escort and Egyptologist for our excursion to the pyramids on the Giza Plateau on the southwestern edge of the city.

On the bus, Layla introduced our security guard who would be with us on the excursion. He had a small machine pistol under his coat—ever so discreet. How can a machine pistol be discreet? A more relevant question is why would anyone going to the pyramids, where it is hot, be wearing a sport coat.

The drive through Cairo to the pyramids is hard to describe. There was a great deal of traffic, goats in the street, and truly ugly buildings. Then there was the trash, trash, trash. There also butcher shops where animals were being killed and prepared for an upcoming feast. We passed miles of what Layla called squatter buildings. They are perhaps seven or eight stories tall and not built well at all; they are essentially cement frames filled in with red brick.

It took us close to an hour to get to the pyramids that are set on a slight rise or plateau; as such they are separated from the encroachment of civilization, but not by much. At the entrance to the plateau, Layla stepped off the bus to purchase our tickets to enter the pyramid area. It is partitioned off from Cairo itself. When she returned to the air-conditioned bus she took time to tell us something of the history of the pyramids. My thought at the time was that she was not telling us anything we did not already know. Perhaps it was new to some of the people in our group.

Layla told us was that we could go inside the main pyramid of Khufu and if we thought we could manage it physically, we should do it. I had not originally planned to do it, but she convinced me I should give it a try. Mrs. C. declined.

The climb to the main burial chamber of the Great Pyramid is indeed difficult. When you enter the pyramid, you go into a small hall, more like a cave, but at least you can stand up. Next, you enter a small, steeply inclined shaft that is only about four feet high. There are handrails and the floor is wooden, like a gangway, with periodic cross boards for stability. This shaft is about 130 feet long and going up is not easy. This shaft opens up into another long steep corridor called the Great Gallery, where you continue to climb. But here you climb standing up. Finally, there is an opening about three-and-a-half feet high and perhaps six feet wide that takes you into the main burial chamber. This opening is only about 12 feet long.

The Kings (burial) Chamber measures approximately 30' x 16', is 18' high, and is made entirely of pink granite. It has its flat roof (composed of nine huge granite blocks) that supports the more than 400 tons of stones above. To support this immense weight, the builders constructed five stress-relieving chambers above the one we were in. In the 4,000 years since their creation, only one small crack has developed in the ceiling slabs. I wonder how they know this.

The King's Chamber is really just an empty space with an empty granite sarcophagus at one end that is broken. It is not worth the effort. You're not supposed to take pictures in the chamber. In fact, they won't let you take cameras inside the pyramid. That said, people have cell phones with cameras that they carry in their pockets. They were taking pictures—of what, I don't really know.

I decided to leave. Fortunately, I did not have a problem with people coming up as I was going down. There weren't any.

It was good to be back outside in the fresh air. Although, the air inside was not as bad as I had expected.

The Pharaoh's Curse came the next morning. When I woke up my butt was so sore I could hardly walk. The climb up to the Kings Chamber had strained muscles I never knew I had.

2. Things Mechanical

When things have gone awry in our travels, they have often been related to things mechanical. Sometimes these events have been serious and sometimes not. This chapter chronicles a few of those mechanical incidents.

<u>On Our Final Approach</u>

We were on an Air France flight in route to Papeete in Tahiti when we awoke to an announcement on the plane's PA ". . . On our final approach."

"Wow," I thought, "I slept for eight hours; I must have really been beat."

I looked out the window and thought, "What are all these lights? This looks like L.A. Shouldn't we be over the Pacific?" What are we doing landing in LA? This isn't where we're supposed to be!"

We were indeed landing at LAX. As we touched down, there were emergency vehicles, fire engines and crash trucks all along the runway. This was not a good sign. As we raced along the runway and the brakes were applied, the crash trucks raced down the taxiway parallel to our aircraft with lights flashing. Fortunately, we landed without incident and the crash vehicles were not needed.

Apparently, although we didn't know it at the time, our flight to Papeete from L.A. had run into trouble shortly after takeoff; our Air France 747 had lost an engine. (It did not fall off. It just stopped working.) Unbeknownst to us, we had spent an hour or so dumping fuel out over the Pacific before returning to LA. This was just a precaution, in case we had an incident landing at LAX. I am sure the fish were not pleased about our dumping fuel, or any boats that might have rained down on.

Why didn't we know what was going on? It was an Air France flight. All the announcements were in French—except, "We are on our final approach."

Our trip had begun the previous evening when we had left Seattle in route to L.A. We arrived in L.A. on time and made our way to the International Terminal, where we checked in with Air France. We had no checked luggage, only carry-ons. This would prove to be a good thing. As it turned out, we had boarded an existing flight, one from Paris to Papeete. We were late leaving L.A., departing a bit after midnight. Once in the air, we thought we were set.

We Had Not Been Anywhere

Once back on the ground in LA and off the main runaway, our aircraft was towed to the gate. It was here that we learned what had happened. We then spent the next two hours sitting in the plane while the ground crew tried to determine whether or not the engine could be repaired and we could be sent on our merry way. While we were waiting, we were asked to fill out immigration forms for re-entry into the United States, in case we had to get off the plane. We might not have been anywhere, but we had left US airspace so we had to fill out Customs forms. The form asked for countries visited — I filled in "USA". If anyone had read it they would not understand. I wonder if astronauts have to fill out Immigration and Customs forms when they land, after all they do leave US airspace.

When it was decided that we could not proceed to Tahiti, we were told that Air France would put us up for the night (what was left of it) at hotels near the airport. At least we could get a little sleep, some food and a shower; otherwise it was going to be a potentially fragrant day.

Passengers were put up at various hotels adjacent to LAX; we ended up at the Holiday Inn Crowne Plaza. We checked in about 5:30 a.m. and were given breakfast and lunch coupons. Finding rooms for this many people on the spur of the moment must have been a logistical nightmare.

When I got up, I called Air France and learned that a new, different actually, plane was being brought in—from Paris. Our scheduled departure was six o'clock that evening with an expected arrival time in Papeete of 11:00 p.m. I had told the Air France representative that a large number of passengers on our flight were scheduled to be on a cruise that was supposed to leave Papeete at 6 o'clock that evening. I wanted to think that Air France would advise the ship of our predicament. After all, Papeete is not that big.

After talking to Air France, I called Windstar Cruises and learned that they were very much aware of our problem, and that they would be holding the ship for us. Super! The ship we were on, the Wind Song, was fairly small, and somewhere between 30 and 50 couples scheduled for the cruise were on our flight.

After lunch at the hotel, we headed back to the airport for our 3 o'clock check-in (there wasn't much else to do.) When we got to the airport, there was a substantial line at the Air France counter. (I guess some people just like to stand in line; we sat and read our books.) The actual check-in didn't start until 3:30 or so and we didn't get in line until sometime after 4 p.m. While in line, we met several couples who were on our cruise. It was a friendly crowd. While we were checking in, other passengers were checking in for a different Air France flight. Somehow we learned that our flight to Tahiti had appropriated their aircraft, and that the aircraft being flown in from Paris would become theirs.

In spite of our predicament, it seemed, to me at least, that the large number of French people had a somewhat calming effect on the Americans. They seem to accept life's little interruptions with more patience than we Americans. This observation about patience will come to mind when you get to "The Knife" section in a coming chapter.

You Are Less Crabby If You've Been Fed

When you are waiting in line you tend to notice things; I noticed that the passengers for Japan Airlines

(JAL) next to us at Air France had to send all their luggage and carry-ons through a special, very large X-ray machine. The machine attendant, an older woman, seemed far more concerned about keeping the throng of Air France passengers from encroaching on her (JAL) space than actually looking at the X-rays of the luggage. It would appear passing luggage through this X-ray machine is some sort of ritual or formality that JAL requires of its passengers.

While we were standing in line, Air France representatives were handing out food coupons for the airport snack shops, I guess people with food in their mouths are less crabby.

When it was our turn at the counter, we decided to check two of our three pieces of carry-on luggage because we now knew the interior configuration of our plane (it was not good for carry-ons). Theoretically, our plane was only going one place. Where else could our bags go? In retrospect, I think this was a good idea.

I was also a bit surprised that both our aircraft, the original and the one we were now on, were 747-200s; I thought most of Air France's aircraft would be Airbus planes. Apparently not.

Once at the departure gate, the same one as the previous night, we got to wait some more. We were certainly getting good at this waiting business.

The resumption of Air France flight #70 to Papeete left the ground around 6:30 p.m. This time we stayed awake for most of the flight. I presume we did not want any more surprises. During the flight we were shown two movies, neither of which we were able to catch the title of. The first one had Sean Penn in it and seemed to be about low-class people who yelled a lot. We just watched it; we didn't have our headphones plugged in. The second one was French and had subtitles; it seemed to have innumerable plot twists, so much so that there were no good guys and you felt that all the characters in the film should be shot (which most of them were). It must be a French thing. On a positive note, the food, with complimentary wine, was very good.

We arrived at the Papeete-Faaa Airport around 10:45 that evening. On our arrival, we were given leis and serenaded by a Tahitian musical group just inside the terminal. The music was not what we needed. I presume the singers had not been told about our travails, or if they had, they did not care, why would they. We were tired and it was hot and humid and we did not want to hear their any music. Can you tell that we were crabby—even though we had been fed? We kept our mouths shut.

Once inside the terminal, we got to fill out more forms (this is why you always carry a pen when traveling) and wait for at least 45 minutes for our uneventful meeting with the Immigration official. It is my considered opinion that our time in line was a ploy by Air France to give them more than ample time to unload the baggage.

Once past Immigration, we grabbed our bags and headed for the Customs counter. They were two different things. There was only one customs agent and he did not seem too concerned about much of anything, so when there was a break in his activities, I asked if we could go on through to the outside, because all we had was carry-ons. He just nodded and we went.

Wasn't Mr. Christian on the Bounty?

Once outside the baggage/customs area we found several cruise line agents underneath a sign that read, "*Wind Song.*" The Wind Song is a four-masted motor sailing yacht. This was a very pleasant sight, indeed: We were expected. We were welcomed with more leis and one of the agents, Christian, took our luggage and then put us on a bus to take us to the ship. We soon departed for the ship. Christian, I thought, was an appropriate name considering where we were—in Tahiti, getting on a sailing vessel, which, fortunately for us, was not named *Bounty*. A mutiny would not be a good thing. Nonetheless, Mr. Christian as I chose to call him seemed genuinely glad to see us, as we were him. This was good news. The not so good news was that because of the aircraft problem we would miss our first port of call.

When we boarded the Wind Song, moored along the Papeete waterfront, it was well past midnight, but nonetheless, we were given refreshing drinks and ushered into the lounge where we checked in with some pleasant folks who did not make us wait. A pleasant change of pace. We were then shown to our cabin, and our bags arrived within minutes. We were exhausted and were asleep as soon as our heads touched the pillow. Shortly thereafter, the ship left the dock and headed out to sea.

Around three o'clock, I was awakened by a moving bed—we were at sea. Hmm, this might not be a good sign.

When morning arrived and I got up to shower, Shirley said she was not feeling well—understandable. The ship was rocking and rolling. Through the portholes I could see that we were experiencing some rough weather and were sailing through some very heavy seas, with 10-15-foot swells. Undeterred, I headed up on deck to look for coffee and some food. Out on deck by the pool I found, Mr. Christian and the coffee I was looking for. That was the good news. The bad news was that I had difficulty keeping the cup under the spout on the pot. I could see that the weather was not good; we had wind, rain and the seas were heavy indeed. From Mr. Christian, I learned that a weather front was passing through and it was an El Niño year so some rough weather was to be expected. Wonderful. I went forward where I could watch the bow crash into the waves. Shirley came on deck only to get a hot chocolate and then returned to the room.

Are We Stuck Out Here

A day later, we approached the island of Bora Bora, our second port-of-call by sea. It was surrounded by low clouds. Along the south side of the lagoon, the clouds took on an eerie green color from the light reflecting off the shallow water. Entering the lagoon from the west, we anchored near the village of Vaitape. The weather was still quite stormy, giving the cliffs above us an imposing, albeit dramatic appearance.

All that you have heard about how beautiful Bora Bora has been inadequate. It is beyond words.

We had an excursion scheduled for the morning called a "Shark's Breakfast." While the weather was clearer than it had been, it was still far from ideal—it was a bit windy and there were lots of clouds. Nonetheless it was gorgeous.

We headed out after breakfast and were pleased to discover that our excursion was to be a combination of shark feeding, snorkeling, and sting-ray feeding—a true adventure.

Our excursion boat was typical of the islands, a dugout of sorts, long and slender with just enough room to sit two abreast. It had an out-rigger, which I was told is always on the left (excuse me, port side) of the boat—for stability. Stability was something I saw as very important considering the chop on the lagoon. There were 10 of us in the boat as we headed out to meet the sharks. The boat was powered by an outboard motor that, about halfway out to the shark-feeding area, all of a sudden began to emit a high-pitched scream. This was not good. Our guide, or more accurately, excursion leader, Johann, seemed concerned at first, but then when he was unable to discern what was causing the squeal, simply muffled it with his shirt, and we proceeded on our way. I had flashbacks of our Air France flight. On the good side, there was a second boat that could tow us back should we become stranded.

We reached the appropriate spot a mile or two offshore but still within the lagoon and scurried out of the boat into the water. In order to provide breakfast for the sharks, we had to entice them to join us—this enticement was chumming (tossing blood and fish guts into the water). This idea seem questionable to me.

The water was about four to five feet deep, and Johann stretched a rope between two rocks just beneath the surface in water. We then became observers rather than active participants in the shark feeding. We held on to the rope as four black-tipped sharks about four feet long nibbled on bits of fish Johann pulled out of a bucket that he held above water. As the sharks were being fed, there were a large number of interlopers, other fish that wanted some of the *really* good stuff that was being dished out. One or two of the interlopers became breakfast for the sharks themselves. When we ran out of chum the sharks drifted off, and we headed out to the reef for some snorkeling time. The water on the reef was quite shallow in places and there was a great deal of coral. Knowing that coral can be quite sharp, *careful* was the watchword. Blood in the water attracts sharks. The snorkeling was very good and there were lots of fish.

After we climbed back in the boat, we headed to a spot with a sandy bottom in hopes of finding some stingrays. We did. Once again we, the observers, started out on a rope stretched out underwater. Just observing didn't last long, for we were soon surrounded by lots of rays looking for food and, seemingly, affection too. They were like kittens, soft gray things rubbing up against you. They gave new meaning to the phrase "in your face." I did learn one important lesson: stingrays should be fed like horses, with an open palm, not with your fingers. While feeding one, I felt its gum (they don't have teeth) clamp down on my fingernails. Oops. I quickly removed my hand to make sure everything was still there. It was. We spent quite a bit of time playing with the rays; they were a lot of fun.

After our time with the rays, the plan was for us to meet the rest of the ship's passengers (and crew) on a *motu* (islet) along the main channel in the lagoon for lunch. As we approached the *motu* we could see that there was no one there. We later learned that the captain had sent the first-mate out to check on the conditions on the *motu* and he reported back that the wind on the *motu* would have sandblasted the passengers. Not good. Our alternative was delicious, a BBQ lunch on board the ship. The grill was placed outside on the deck, but we ate indoors due to the wind. In any event, lunch was super.

Land Rovers

Another Bora Bora excursion was into the outback of the island in 4-wheel drive Land Rovers. The word outback is a misnomer. Perhaps a better term would be out-up, up the peaks of the island. This should be enjoyable; it was a beautiful day after all—just what you'd want from the South Pacific—blue skies, a few puffy clouds and, not too hot.

We were met at the dock by four Land Rovers, each of which seats eight in the back and one up front next to the driver. Our driver was named Jackson and he was one fierce looking fellow, very dark, clad in only an orange floral pareo (sarong) around his waist, with bright green wild grasses in his hair. He was a lot of fun.

Our ride up to the peaks of the island can best be described as *Indiana Jones on Bora Bora*. We, in the Rovers, climbed up into the hills to an old gun emplacement left by the Navy during WW II when over 5,000 men were stationed on the island. (It's hard to imagine that many people here.) From our vantage point, we looked down into varied colors of the water in the lagoon. Breathtaking.

Leaving the gun emplacement, we headed north and higher on the coastal road (the only road), stopping along the way to pick up some French bread baked by a Chinese family for the locals. Towards the northern end of the island we headed up another hill (on an extremely rocky road) to a failed restaurant site overlooking the lagoon. About two thirds of the way up our Rover lost one of its wheel-drive shaft connections. The other Rovers were way ahead of us. Jackson advised them of our predicament by radio and then we all headed up to top of the hill or mountain, depending on one's perspective, on foot. Our broken Rover would have to be fixed before the other Rovers could get down to the main road—we were in their way. Fortunately for all, the driver of the first Rover was also the mechanic.

By now we had noticed that on this trip, there seemed to be an issue of some sort with anything related to mechanical transportation. Hmmmmm.

The view from the top of the hill, from amid a grove of pines, was what we came to the South Pacific to see. Here, the real peaks of the island are almost un-scalable and are more than 2,500 feet high.

While we enjoyed the view, we consumed a good amount of Polynesian pineapple. I am inclined to say that the pineapple here is better than Hawaiian pineapple, but perhaps it's just the surroundings.

Eventually our Rover was fixed, so we walked back down to it and then headed off around to the eastern side of the island.

Back on board the ship, the Captain announced that he was expecting some rough seas in route to Moorea "so those inclined to sea-sickness should probably prepare." There were (free) seasick pills available throughout the voyage just outside the ship's doctor's office.

We weighed anchor while we were having lunch and we were soon headed out of the lagoon into the deep blue waters of the South Pacific. (Sounds fabulous doesn't it?)

Bora Bora has only one opening in the reef because it has only one primary spot where the freshwater from the island runs out into the ocean. The fresh water kills the reef and thus makes an opening.

Once out at sea and away from Bora Bora, the seas did indeed pick up and the atmosphere onboard became subdued to say the least. I bought some acupressure wristbands for Shirley but she seemed more comfortable lying in bed. I, on the other hand, was on deck thoroughly enjoying the bow crashing into the oncoming swells.

When dinnertime came, Shirley went to the dining room with me and ordered her dinner, but was feeling rather poorly in spite of the seasick precautions. For me, I found it difficult to eat when you need to hold your plate on the table. Before her entrée arrived she told our waiter that what she really wanted was dessert so he brought her some. She was able to finish most of it when her entrée arrived. After a couple of bites, she decided to head back down to the cabin. For me, I fight seasickness with a full stomach. The dining room was almost empty.

Back in the room I read for a while before *attempting* to sleep. I found it very difficult to sleep with the rocking and rolling of the ship—I felt like I was in a sauté pan, being shuffled and tossed. In fact, I went up on deck a couple of times during the night because it seemed smoother up there.

I was told the seas aren't normally this heavy in this part of the world—it was *El Niño*. The weather had been severe enough to rip one of the ship's sails. Not good.

Sparkplugs

After our cruise we had arranged to stay a few nights on the island of Moorea 11 or so miles to the west of Tahiti. Waking up on Moorea in French Polynesia is indeed waking up in paradise. Our hotel room looked out over the water, which we found very calming. The air was calm and the water was as smooth as glass. Our room's deck extended out over the water and we could see black spiny sea urchins in clusters next to the shore. They seem to "come out" at dusk and roam around the area during the night. They're shy in the daylight hours.

After breakfast, we stopped at the rental car desk at the hotel to inquire about renting a car to explore the island. Not only were the cars expensive to rent for the day, but also, there were none available. When we got back to the room, we called the Albert rent-a-car office (which was more or less across the road from the hotel next to ours) to see if they had a car. Joe, who answered the phone (we were to learn his name later), said yes he had a car. He said he'd pick us up at 9 o'clock.

We were waiting under the hotel's *porté cochere* when Robert, a fellow we had met the day before, showed up. We asked if he there to give us a ride and he said, "No." Even so, Robert was friendly and ended up giving us a ride down to the rental car office anyway.

Joe asked if we wanted to pay by cash or credit card, and we said cash. Because we were paying with cash he said we could pay when we got back. The price was fairly reasonable. He gave us a receipt, even though we had not paid, and the keys to the car. The only car. The car, as it turned out, was probably the worst car I have ever driven. It did not accelerate well in first or second gear—first was worse. This car needed new spark plugs more than any car on the planet. Third and fourth gear were, at first, impossible to find and it almost seemed like there was a place for a fifth and sixth gear but they weren't there. You opened the driver's side door by reaching through the window and opening it from the outside. The spot where the radio was supposed to be was just a tangle of loose wire ends. There were side rear view mirror holders, but no mirrors. We decided our trip around the island was going to be interesting if nothing else. It seemed that our transportation karma was holding true to form.

Our first stop on our island circle tour was the Rotui Juice Distillery, where Shirley had found some things she wanted to buy. It was difficult to purchase anything at the distillery because there was some sort of tour group there, and getting to the counter with the tour members wanting their free rum punches was very difficult. It is never a good idea to get between people and free booze.

Next, we stopped at the Bali-Hai shops, where we found Robert (again). He was in his wife's black pearl shop. In talking to him, we discovered that we had not rented one of Albert's rental cars but Joe's personal car (this explained a lot). All the real rental cars were gone. Robert said we could exchange it for one of the real rental cars he had there, but this would involve filling out a bunch of papers, so we decided to go on with what we had after all.

We looked at the black pearls in Robert's wife's shop, but decided not to purchase any. They just didn't seem to be the right thing, and most of the nice ones seemed to be running better than $800. They just seemed, for the most part, uninspired and overpriced.

Our next stop was *La Maison Blanc*, a shop in a plantation house along the road. They had neat stuff—

some of which we bought for gifts. The people in the shop recommended a place next door for a pizza lunch. Well, the pizza was different, if nothing else. Instead of dough, they used a pastry base. Shirley and I had two different kinds, but the difference was minimal.

After lunch, we headed east on our clockwise tour around the island. Along the northeast side we encountered a hill. Uh-oh. On the incline the car kept going slower, and slower, and slower—I kept downshifting and downshifting—eventually into first gear. I had serious doubts that the car would make it up the hill. Obviously, we weren't going to take this car up into the mountains to see the waterfalls.

As we drove around the island, it was like going back in time; Moorea is fairly rural to begin with, but as we got away from the more touristy northeastern shore, it became even more so. We supposed that this is what Kauai was like 20 or 30 years ago.

We eventually took the car back to Joe. I told him I would send him spark plugs for the car when I got back home. I did and I hope they helped.

No Crocodiles

We were on a river cruise on the Nile a couple of years after the Arab Spring Egyptian Revolution, during a calm period, and were docked in Aswan in southern Egypt. We had scheduled a late afternoon excursion, a felucca ride on the Nile. A felucca is the type of sailboat used on the Nile. Unfortunately, when we boarded the felucca there was no wind. Not to be undone by this situation, our skipper—I doubt they are called "skipper" in Egypt—arranged to have another boat with a motor tow us. Fine. Obviously we had no motor on our felucca. From Aswan, we headed south towards the Lower Aswan Dam. The larger High (Aswan) Dam is further south and holds back Lake Nasser.

In the middle of the river here, there is an island called Elephantine. The island is about two-thirds of a mile long and was once considered to be the border between Egypt and Nubia. In fact, our boatmen were Nubian; they have very dark skin, much more so than the Egyptians.

It is believed that the island received its name because it was a major ivory trading center. In fact, it was a major trading post of many commodities. More likely, the name came from some large boulders on the edge of the island that resembled bathing elephants.[1] There are gardens on the island, a small hotel, and a few very upscale homes.

We went as far south as we could, to the dam, before heading north along the west side of the island. Here we were able to see a nature park that seemed a bit odd for this part of Africa, and the compound and mausoleum of Aga Khan—there has been more than one—set high above the river on the west bank.

The Aga Khan was and is the spiritual leader, the Imām of the Ismailis, a Shi'ite sect based principally in India but with followers around the world. The

---

[1] http://www.touregypt.net/elephantine.htm

mausoleum is a very elegant pink granite structure built in the late 1950s, and it resembles the Fatimid tombs in Cairo. (Fatimid is a form of architecture developed in this region before the year 1000.) Members of this sect consider themselves to be the direct spiritual descendants of the Fatimid dynasty that ruled much of northern Africa between 909 and 1171. The Mausoleum has an excellent view, including Aga Khan's white villa on the river below. I can't say I understand why we want the final resting place of the dead to have a view. They are not going to see it.

From what I have read I believe all Aga Khans are extremely wealthy. On his birthday in 1945, he received his weight in diamonds, which he then distributed to his followers. It seems he was a large man, so his followers must have been quite pleased.

After the Aga Khan's death, his widow lived in the island villa three months of the year, and when she was in residence it is said that she had a fresh red rose placed on the marble tomb every day. When Egyptian roses could not be found, they were flown in from Paris by private jet. She died in July 2000.

I mentioned that our felucca was being towed. We were just past the north end of the Elephantine Island when the wind came up and our skipper thought we could sail. Ha! No sooner had we put the sail up, the wind died again. Now we had a problem. Our towboat had cast off and could not come back to us because its engine had died. Not only did it have a dead engine, it was caught in the current and being pulled further and further away from us.

One of our boatmen dove into the water to swim over to the other boat to see if he could get the engine started.

The Nile, in times past, was known for crocodiles. In the town of Kom Ombo, just a little north of Aswan, there is a Crocodile Museum with a number of preserved and/or mummified crocodiles. Good thing there were no crocodiles now.

While our boatman was a decent swimmer, he could not catch up to the towboat. Eventually he made it but was exhausted. And he could not get the motor started either.

I will shorten the story by saying that our remaining boatman was able to shout to another boat that was kind enough to tow us back across the river to our dock.

3. Transportation

Transportation is the theme of this chapter. Getting around, let alone to your destination, can sometimes be challenging at home, but in unfamiliar surroundings, more so.

No Shared Machine Guns

When we were on our Nile river cruise and had left Luxor we headed north towards Nagaa Hammadi. Nagaa Hammadi is very much off the regular path for tourists, onboard they referred to it as "the frontier."

Along the way we stopped at the Nile town of Qena to pick up our security personnel. Our guards boarded our boat armed with automatic weapons and what looked to be a .30 caliber machine gun on wheels. While we expected the additional security, what I did not expect was that there was already security staff on board the boat with their own machine gun. They got off and took their machine gun with them. Apparently, you do not share machine guns.

The new guards were authorized for the region into which we were going. Apparently, we were truly headed into the *frontier*. The security staff that had boarded was stationed below the aft deck, where we had lunch on most days.

We reached Nagga Hammadi in the early afternoon. Here we created a convoy for the 75-mile drive to Abydos, the holy site of Osiris, Lord of the Netherworld. Our convoy consisted of our mini-bus, a van for the Italians, a car for the Australians, and a lead and trailing army vehicle, with armed security.

Why all the security? The reason is that back in 1997, a religious faction of some sort killed some tourists, and the government wants to make sure it does not happen again. We liked being kept safe too.

About two-thirds of the way to Abydos we had to change our guards/escorts because we were moving into a different jurisdiction.

The Temple of Osiris is as spectacular, particularly on the outside, as were many of the other temples we had visited. The inside is awesome as well. The pictures on the walls here are quite well preserved. Not so much so the erect penis of Horace in the "Divine Impregnation Hall of Horace and Isis." It is the only part that has been defaced It has been chipped away. Can't say I understand that or The Divine Impregnation Hall? An interesting name.

Not Much Runway

The airport of St. Barth's in the Caribbean is one of world's most interesting airports. People flying to St. Barth's usually connect in St. Martin, and the aircraft that makes the flight are usually small 12-seaters.

When we boarded our aircraft in St. Martin we were informed that we would be "flying at an altitude of 1,500 feet and that the flight would take about 10 minutes." We were also advised that the approach would likely be a bit bumpy. No kidding.

At St. Barth's, landing is an adventure. We came in with full flaps to slow our approach speed, and you pretty much feel like the nose of the plane is pointed at the ground. You approach the runway between two mountains, clearing the road below by 20 to 30 feet, and then coming down onto the runway which slopes towards the sea. Once on the ground, engines were reversed and we backed up from the end of the runway to taxi to the gate.

Customs here seemed to be a mere formality.

You Can't Bring A Dog On This Plane

Leaving St. Barth's was also interesting. We got to the airport a bit early for our flight and when went to check in the agent said we could take an earlier flight if we wanted. We said, "Sure."

The plane was the same small 12-seater we had come in on, but there was room for the two of us. We placed our bags in the luggage compartment and climbed aboard.

Our departure was delayed a few minutes while waiting for two people who appeared at the gate at the last minute with two dogs, which they stuffed into a carry-on bag. When they boarded, the pilot looked around and told them he was unable to depart with dogs in the cabin. They feigned that they did not understand. To shorten the story, a local gendarme (police officer) appeared outside the plane and the people and their dogs got off. They would have to take the ferry to St. Martin. We departed pretty much on schedule.

Taking off from St. Barth's is just as interesting as landing. The pilot takes the plane up the hill you come in over at the west end of the airport, does a U-turn, and then goes full throttle down the hill towards the bay. You can see all of this because there is no door to the cockpit. Once the proper ground speed is attained, the pilot pulls back on the yoke and you soar out over the water. Piece of cake.

Trains – Is There Always a Supplement?

The two phrases "traveling by train" and "traveling by train in Italy" do not necessarily bring to mind the same thing. On one trip to Italy, we did a great deal of the latter, not the former. Starting in Rome, our plan was to use the Italian rail system throughout our trip eventually reaching Milan, our final destination prior to returning to the US.

We arrived in Italy at the Leonardo da Vinci Airport, which is outside of Rome—far outside, on the coast. After clearing Customs, we had to decide, "What's the best way to get into Rome?" In my early travels I used to worry, though not too much, about how I was to get to where I was going from the airport, but in most cities these days, this question seems to have been anticipated, and travelers are provided with alternatives. All you have to do is figure out which option is best for you. Deciphering and evaluating your options can be slightly tricky, but it is generally not too difficult. In this particular situation, we determined that the best way to the main terminal in Rome, the Rome Termini, was by train. Imagine that. Once there, we could walk to our hotel.

I suppose it should be said that prior to embarking on this Italian odyssey, we made an effort to heed the advice of those who had gone before us, those who said, "When in Rome, do as the Romans." This meant learning some Italian. Before we left home, we listened to Italian language tapes each day while driving to work. The unfortunate part of our learning "key words and phrases" was that while we could recognize quite a few Italian words, when we heard them in a different context, we had very little idea what they meant.

At the airport, we followed the pictograms (signs with a picture of a train on them) and thus found the train station (we must be rocket scientists). Since there was a line at the ticket counter, we decided to try the automated ticket dispensers. The first thing the LCD screen on the automated ticket machine asks you to do is pick a language. This is done by touching the appropriate flag on the screen. We chose English, signified by a British flag. My ninth-grade geography teacher, Miss Erb, would be proud. Ideally, the machines give you instructions on how to purchase your tickets. I say ideally because the machines' LCD screens don't quite seem to give you all the information you might need or desire; they simply ask questions like "Where do you want to go?" The real instructions are on the side of the machine. These "How to" instructions (in several languages) are what is really necessary to make the machine work. Once you have selected your destination, the machine asks, "How many people are traveling?" we punched the "Two" button. It asked, "Smoking or non?" We punched the "non" button. It said, "Give me some money" (it was about $7.50 per person). We did. The machine then printed our tickets, *slowly*, and *slowly* gave us our change. According to the instructions on the side of the machine, we were supposed to have been asked whether or not we wanted first or second class. We weren't. Perhaps there is only first class to Rome. We will likely never know.

Above the train platform there was a reader board that displayed the *Partenz* (departure) schedule. We determined that the next train to Rome left in just a few minutes. I should mention that the word "*partenz*" was not a word found on our language tapes. It was just one of those things you pick up along the way, like "*uscita*" for exit, a word that could be very handy in case of fire. We made it through the automatic turnstile to the train platform by sticking our tickets in a little slot marked with an arrow, they were stamped and the turnstile let us pass. Just like the subway in US cities. When our train arrived, we boarded the first first-class car, after all, that's the only type of ticket the machine would sell us.

At some point before we arrived, a conductor came through and punched our tickets. Entertainment along the way was provided by a couple of young Romans who put on a show of lustful infatuation.

One of our first major discoveries upon arriving in Rome was the restroom furnishings, or the lack thereof.

The toilets at the train station had no seats, and no toilet paper. I mention this because it is part of the Italian train experience. I wonder if there is a black market for toilet seats that I am unaware of.

From the station, we were able to walk to our hotel and, as it turns out, we found almost everything in Rome based on its proximity to the train station. In fact, in each of the cities we visited, the train station became our main point of reference; everything was located in relationship to the train station.

In Rome, you can purchase train tickets from almost any travel agency or from a kiosk at the station. During the process of purchasing tickets from a kiosk, we learned a great deal about the Italian train system. We wanted to go to Florence so after selecting our destination of Firenze, we had a choice of the type of train regular or high-speed train. We selected the high-speed. It would get us there in approximately two hours. Of course, there is a "*supplement*" for the faster train (approximately $20.00). Next, we had to decide the class of service we wanted, first or second. We decided on first class even though it was a little more expensive, but it ensured that the cars would be air-conditioned. Our next option was whether or not we wanted reserved seats. We were under the impression that the run between Rome and Florence was quite popular, so we decided to go for the seat reservations or *prenotazione*. You guessed it; there was a "*supplement*" for the ticket.

The trains/subways beneath Rome are actually a good way of getting around the city. Although the network is not extensive, there are just two primary lines, the trains and the stations are in fairly good shape, better than many of the ones in New York and Chicago. We use them whenever practical.

On the day we were to leave for Florence, our train was scheduled to leave at 13:05 (all European train times use a 24 hour clock), so we arrived at the train station at about 12:45 p.m. hoping this would give us enough time to find our train, our car, and our seats. Once inside the main station, we read the *Partenz* board to determine which *binario* (track) our train was on. We found the track and checked the destination on the reader boards above the train to doubly ensure we had found the correct one. We are, indeed, experienced train travelers. Our car was at the far end of a very long train, portending things to come. Once we found the car and our seats, we were very pleased to discover that we had a whole compartment to ourselves. The compartment was quite comfortable. It was air-conditioned, and even though it was an unattractive color, it did have a large window. There was a glass partition separating us from the corridor and we took this as a hint that certain activities where probably not advisable. We left on time, contrary to rumors we had heard about the trains frequently running late.

The train was truly a high-speed train, nearing speeds of 100 mph. I was a bit surprised at the number of tunnels we went through on our way north out of Rome. Because of our speed we noticed a substantial compression in our ears each time we entered a tunnel. I don't think babies would like this.

After quite a while a conductor came through and punched our tickets, assuring us that we were on the right train. He was followed shortly thereafter by a man with a cart selling assorted food snacks and drinks. We had read that the food on the trains is not what you would call terrific, so we had eaten an early lunch prior to leaving Rome; we let him pass.

We arrived in Florence right around 3 p.m. (excuse me: 15:00) and from the station we walked a couple blocks to the auto rental agency. We weren't staying in Florence, but in the town of Prato about 14 kilometers west.

Push the Red Button

I need to digress here for a moment. You may wonder why Florence is Florence to some and to others it is Firenze. I looked it up and this is what I found. "It was called *Florentia* in Latin, then *Fiorenza* in Old Italian, then *Firenze*. The names foreigners call it by, like Florence in English and French and *Florenz* in German, are closer to the original, probably because they were mostly used in writing."[2]

Back in Florence, obtaining the rental car should not be a problem, just walk a few blocks. No problem. At least in theory. To a non-Florentine, finding anything in Florence can be a challenge, even with a map. The reason is that the streets frequently change names. The *via Il Prato* in one block is the *via Florlanini* in another. This

---

[2] https://www.quora.com/Why-is-Firenze-called-Florence-in-English

was done, or so I was told, to confuse invaders. It must work, for as a tourist invader, I was confused.

We got our car and some instructions on how to get to the A11 highway. The A11 would take us to Prato, where we had arranged to stay in a bed & breakfast that is housed in a former Medici family villa.

The A11 motorway connects Florence to Pisa and starts just outside of Florence. To get on the highway, I pulled up to a gate. It wasn't really a toll booth, but there was a box on a pole next to the gate. The box obviously had a speaker and a big red button. There was no slot or anything that looked like it would spit out a ticket. I was unsure what to do. I said, "*Buongiorno*," to the box. Nothing happened. I pushed the red button. From the bottom of the machine, a card emerged. I took the card, said, "grazie," to the machine and the gate went up and off we went.

Push the red button.

I think we Americans are far too used to having instructions telling us what to do.

The Stazioni

Generally speaking, you do not find a plethora of services at Italian train stations, the *stazioni*. You might find a place to buy a magazine or a paper, perhaps a bite to eat. Perhaps not. Depending on the size of the station, if it's a large one, you might find a tourist information office, but generally not the services you would find at an airport, such as a rental car desk.

We planned to spend a week in Tuscany, though not specifically in Florence. We were staying in a villa in the town of Prato, about 12 miles west of Florence, so we needed a car. If you were staying in Florence, you probably wouldn't need one. More to the point, you probably wouldn't want one, as driving in the city can be tricky. Shirley's word is "hair-raising". On the days we spent sightseeing in Florence, we took the train in from Prato, partly because one of the best places to park in Florence is at the train station. So what would be the point in not taking the train?

The first day we "trained" into Florence, we bought our tickets in Prato. Unfortunately, we didn't think to get round-trip tickets, so when we arrived in Florence, we needed to purchase our return tickets from the ticket vending machine. We were experts with these machines by now.

The "facilities" at some train stations can be rather limited. At the Prato station, the toilets were of the ancient Roman kind, two foot indentation next to a hole in the floor (at least in the men's room). This must have something to do with train stations, because most restrooms have toilets. Some even have toilet seats.

During one of our excursions into Florence, we bought our tickets for the next leg of our trip, Venice. In doing so, we found out that making reservations is a sometimes a separate step from buying tickets—at least it was then. Reservations meant going to a separate window where you get to stand in line again. The line at that window moved imperceptibly, if at all, so we decided to make our reservations in Prato. While there was no line in Prato, there was also no English, so I used my truly meager Italian language skills.

The Hidden Train Station

One of the things we most wanted to do while in Tuscany was visit the Cinque Terra on the west coast of Italy. Our plan was to drive to La Spezia from Prato and from there take the coastal train to the five Cinque Terra towns that are inaccessible by car. La Spezia turned out not to be a town, but a city, much larger than we had thought. As a result, finding the train station proved to be a task that could not have been accomplished without Divine help. Why would they hide the train station? Today, having GPS would make it easier. In theory. But then again, perhaps not.

The trip along the coast doesn't take long, nor is it what I would call *scenic*, as it is almost entirely through tunnels.

We had only planned on going as far as Vernazza (the fourth town), but changed our minds in route and continued on to Monterosso, the northernmost of the five towns. (It doesn't really seem to matter which town you go to; the price to any of the towns is the same.) Once we got off the train, we bought our return tickets to La Spezia; this ticket, should anybody check it, would allow us to stop off at any or all of the other towns on the way back.

At our destination I checked the schedule to make sure I knew the departure times for the next few trains headed south. After exploring Monterosso, which to some might seem a bit "touristy," we returned to the station to catch the train for our eight-minute ride to Vernazza. It is possible to hike along the coast, but it's a good two-hour walk, and the trails can be rough.

Vernazza is probably the most picturesque of all the Cinque Terra villages. It has a stone tower overlooking a small harbor and cove for swimming (the harbor and swimming cove are one and the same). It also has a very small train station. We wandered the streets of Vernazza for a short time before returning to the station only to find that the next passenger train wasn't for another hour. We went back down into the town to see if there was anything we had missed. Apparently not much.

At the station once again, we found that we could foretell the coming of a train, usually a freight train, by the ringing of a bell over the tunnel and the sudden rush of wind preceding it. The wind, not a breeze, is quite welcome if it is hot.

When at last the passenger train finally arrived, we traveled the seven minutes to Corniglia, where upon exiting the train, we discovered that the town was perched 1,000 feet up the hillside. Not good. With it so hot, we did not make the climb into town, so we'll never know what we missed. While waiting on the platform for the next train, we were surrounded by flowers and an incredible view of Manarola, the next town south, perched on a peninsula jutting out into the Ligurian Sea. It was definitely not a bad way to spend time on a summer afternoon.

The ride to Manarola took just a couple of minutes. Manarola is smaller than Vernazza, and its harbor, if you can call it that, requires the boats, which are kept on dollies in the town, be lowered from a cliff into the cove below. We toured the town in about 20 minutes as we thought there was another train due at 19:20 to take us to the next town, Riomaggiore. Wrongo.

The 19:20 train runs only on festival days. (You'd think after all this time I could read a train schedule. Guess not.) We went back down into town to find food. Train travel makes you hungry.

As I alluded to, theoretically, you are supposed to be able to walk between the towns of the Cinque Terra, but this is not necessarily true. Or true only sometimes. They also say that the walk between Manarola and Riomaggiore (the southernmost town) is the easiest walk, along a path known as the *via del Amore* (road of love). It might be the easiest if you could get to it. Unfortunately, on the day we were there, all access to the path was closed off by high walls and an iron gate. This leaves only the train. When we finally did leave Manarola, it was getting late, so we went back to La Spezia, bypassing Riomaggiore altogether—once again not knowing what we missed. We'll have to go back when we have more time. Rick Steves would probably think that we wimped out. We did.

You Can't Get Too Lost

When we arrived at the station to catch our train to Venice, we found that our car was, as usual, at the far end of the train. I think there must be some sort of Murphy's Law about trains that I am unaware of. Fortunately, Italian train stations are fairly well laid out and they always seem to have plenty of luggage carts on the platform that you can just grab if you need one. They're free, unlike in the US.

We found our car and our seats, but we also found people in them, people from San Francisco. Therefore they spoke English. They were in our seats because people were in their seats. It was a crowded train. Eventually, we got everyone seated, but we were certainly glad we had reserved seats. There were no compartments on this train.

While in route to Venice, we could not help noticing some other Americans a couple of sections behind us. They had two huge suitcases next to their seats, partially blocking the aisle; they should have been placed on the overhead racks. When the snack and drink man came with his cart he couldn't get through. They just responded with, "We can't move them, they're too heavy." How the hell did they get them on the train, with a forklift? Eventually, he gave up trying to get his cart past them and just asked the rest of the people in the car if they wanted anything to eat or drink. Later on during the trip, a much larger snack person came through and pushed the luggage into the area where the people were sitting so he could get by. These people were your typical "obnoxious tourists"— something most responsible people try to avoid becoming.

We arrived in Venice a little before six in the evening and found our way to our hotel; a short walk from the train station. The train station is a key reference point in Venice; all signs point to either *San Marco*, the main square or *Ferrovia*, where they keep the train station. If we got lost, we could in theory find our way back to our hotel. That said, if they tell you, "You can't get too lost in Venice," "they" are wrong.

Prior to leaving Venice, we stopped in at a travel agent's office with a sign in the window that read, "Train Tickets." It was in English—imagine that. The gentleman behind the counter seemed more interested in talking about our camera than in selling us train tickets, but he was very nice nonetheless. These Venetians are a loquacious people. When we finally got around to the tickets, I said (in English), "We want to go to Lake Como on Sunday." He said, "You want to go to Como?" I answered, "Yes."

Well, perhaps not. We (I) did not think of the town called Como. I just thought, Lake Como. I failed to mention that where I really wanted to go was Varenna, on the east side of the lake. He said, "Very good. There is a train that leaves at 12:25 tomorrow afternoon to Milan and continues on to Zurich through Como. You don't even have to change trains in Milan!" It wasn't until later that I realized where we were actually going: Como, not Varenna. Oh well, at least it's on the lake.

To Como

On Sunday morning in Venice we were awakened by the peal of church bells, a not unpleasant way to greet the day. It went on for hours. After we packed and had breakfast, we left our bags at the hotel and set off on one final shopping expedition before heading for the train.

On our way to the station, we bought sandwiches and drinks for our trip. Mrs. C. does not like to go anywhere without food, particularly when she is not sure where her next meal is coming from. At the station, we found our train and our car—you know where—at the far end. Once seated, we immediately broke into our sandwiches. Train travel does make you hungry—even if you haven't left the station.

Once again the train was full, so having assigned seats was really worth the extra money. Without reservations, you could have first-class tickets and be split up, or not even be able to find a seat. Also, for the first-class premium, a few extra dollars, you get nicer cars and a more pleasant rail experience.

The train trip to Como took about four hours, and along the way we got to see quite a lot of country along the way. While at the *Villa Rucellai* in Prato, we had heard that Como was fairly empty this time of year, the real tourist rush starting in July a few weeks away. In route to Milan, we got to see quite a lot of not particularly exciting country, but it gave us a taste of this part of Italy. From Milan to Como the trip is more or less a commuter run of about 20 minutes, and it definitely climbs towards the Alps.

When we got to Como, I called the first place on our list of lodging possibilities, a four-star hotel on the lake, the *Villa Flori*. After the obligatory, "*Lei parla inglese?*" (Do you speak English?), I asked if they had any rooms available. They said, "Yes." I asked how much? They said, "L170,000." (Obviously, this was in a time before the Euro, when the Italian currency was the lira.) Promising. I asked if it had a lake view, and they said. "Yes." I said, "We'll take it. How do we get there?"

We took a taxi to the hotel, which is in a park-like setting along the lake. (This was the first taxi ride of the trip and it felt like a splurge!) When we walked into the hotel, the young lady behind the desk said, "You must be Mr. Chesnutt." She was right: I was. They took our passports and carried our bags to the room. What a luxury. It was nearing the end of our trip, and we were getting tired. We needed some pampering. Our room was small, but it had a beautiful view back across the lake towards Como through floor-to-ceiling windows. We relaxed and thoroughly enjoyed it.

Not wanting to leave the hotel that evening, we had dinner there. We had their version of *Tournedos Rossini* a fabulous steak dish named for the Italian composer Antonio Rossini. When ordering we failed to mention that we wanted the meat at least medium, so when it came it was very rare. This was fine for me, less so for Mrs. C. Shirley ate the more well-done parts of each of our servings. During dinner, we decided to stick to our planned departure on Tuesday and to stay at the *Villa Flori* on Monday night, as well instead of trying to move to a hotel in Varenna. This way it would be easier to get to Milan's Linate Airport in time for our mid-morning flight to London. The trip had worn us out, and going home sounded like a good idea.

I'm Not In Yet

On the evening before our departure from the town of Como, we stopped by the front desk to see if they could arrange for a taxi to pick us up at 6 o'clock the next morning to take us to the train station. They said, "But of course," and called to make the reservation. We were told there would be no one at the desk at six in the morning, so it would be best to check out now, which we did. I asked if we'd be able to get out in the morning and was told, "Yes," they would leave the key in the door.

The next morning we went down to the lobby a little before 6:00 and found that indeed the front door to the hotel was locked, and that the keys were not in the door. Uh-oh.

Fortunately, I found the keys on the front desk and tried a few before I found one that opened the door to the hotel courtyard. With the door opened, I went outside only to find that there was a 10-foot high fence around the driveway and the gates were closed and locked. There was no way out—or in. Our taxi would show up and we couldn't get to it. We looked for another door but they were locked as well, and I really didn't want to go through

20 or so keys to find one that fit. I then took the keys I had left in the main door and headed outside, hoping, "Maybe one of these keys will unlock the gates." I tried each one on an electric slide gate but to no avail. Then I tried them on the padlocked gate. The third key worked. "Yes!"

As I opened the main gate, the electric side gate opened as well. When I went back inside to put the keys on the desk, the taxi arrived. Nice timing. We made it to the station in plenty of time for the 6:26 train to Milan.

We thought our troubles were over. We sat near where, we thought, the front of the train would be when it stopped. This way, when we got off in Milan, we wouldn't have to walk so far with our luggage. Our thinking was flawed.

When the train arrived, the first several cars were mail cars, followed by first-class sleeper cars. We had second-class tickets—after all, it was only a 23-minute ride to Milan, and it was 6 o'clock in the morning. How busy could the train be? Flawed thinking again.

We ran down towards the other end of the train, where people were crowding on only to find the entrance to the car full, as was the entrance to the next car and the next. We were getting concerned—fast. Trains, Italian or not, do not stop at local stations for very long. When I found an entrance we could squeeze into, I got on and I got one of our bags in. The whistle blew. The train was ready to leave. I took the second bag from Mrs. C. and told her to step onto the bottom step. As she got her foot onboard, the whistle blew again. Tweeeet. She pulled herself up but the door couldn't close with part of her still hanging outside the door. She said "I'm not in yet!"

We eventually got both of us in the train, the door closed, and we began to roll. We squeezed past the other folks who were standing at the end of the car. They were mostly young people with big backpacks. We made it to the next car, which was slightly less crowded. Part of the reason for the crowd was that these were sleeper cars, so there were no seats. And at the end of each car there was a restroom, and the sleeper people were queued up to get in for their morning activities.

After a while the crowd thinned out considerably, but no one ever checked our tickets. We stood for the half-hour ride to Milan's central station. At the station, we were some of the first ones off the train, or so it seemed, perhaps it was because of the car we were in, one of the last ones. We grabbed a luggage cart for our bags and began our investigations on how to get to the airport.

To get to the airport, we followed the *uscita* (exit) signs and found one with a picture of an airplane on it. We were looking for the bus to the airport. It was not to be found. However, I did find a cab. We took it and arrived at the Linate Airport in plenty of time, about an hour prior to our scheduled departure. No sweat.

When flying into or out of Milan, you need to pay attention to which airport you need or want. There are three, but the main ones are Linate and Malpensa.

Linate Airport is the city airport of Milan. Due to its vicinity to Milan, it is mainly used for domestic and short-haul international flights.

Malpensa Airport is a little ways out of town and is the main hub for the Italian airline Al Italia and many long-haul overseas international flights.

All Kinds of Noise

We were staying in Positano on the Amalfi coast south of Naples and planned to travel by train from Naples to Venice by train.

We elected to splurge and take a taxi to the train station in Naples. Alternatives seemed complicated and prone to problems. We would have had to: Take a bus or taxi back to Sorrento; then a boat to the Naples port or take the *Circumvesuvia* to the *Stazioni Centrale* in Napoli; and a cab from either the port or the train station to the second Naples train station, *Campi Flegrei*. We had no idea where *Campi Flegrei* was so the taxi was a good plan.

The taxi from Positano was supposed to take two hours, but it was probably closer to three due to the traffic we encountered on the Napoli toll-way. Because our driver spoke excellent English, along the way we learned a lot about Naples and saw quite a bit of it that we might not normally have seen. He had lived in the US for 10 years, but left when his business partner got their business in trouble with the IRS. He said the partner had figured that everybody cheats on their taxes in Italy, so he could do it in the US. Wrongo.

Some of his other comments were that: British tourists aren't very friendly and that Vesuvius isn't really as dormant as the local people are led to believe. He told us that there used to be a funicular that went up the side of the volcano, but it isn't there anymore. He said that there also used to be a number of exclusive homes on the side of the mountain, but now they can't be sold.

He said that in response to problems tourists were having in Naples, there were now a large number of undercover policemen. (Even so, you still don't venture outside the train station at two in the morning.) I can't say this is a good idea in most cities, the US included. Either way I had no plans of doing that.

When we got to the *Campi Flegrei* station, I thought our driver deserved a good tip because the ride turned out to be a very informative.

Inside the station, I checked the posted schedule and found our train was due to depart from track #3. But, just to be on the safe side, I checked with the agent at the window; it was a good thing I did because our train was on *binario quattro* (track 4). I had a feeling that this was going to be an interesting journey.

We sat on the platform for about 40 minutes before a train showed up. As the train was pulling in, I saw that some of the cars had small placards on them saying Venezia, so I presumed it was our train.

There are reader boards over the platforms that are supposed to tell you what the train is, but they didn't work—they were blank. After a while, I approached a train employee and asked, *"Questa treno per Venezia?"* (Is this the train for Venice?)

He said, *"Si."*

Our assigned car was at the end of the train. When we boarded, the conductor checked out reservation slip and kept our rail passes, saying they would be returned to us in the morning. Our compartment was small, but at least it was private. It had two bunks, an upper and a lower, as well as a tiny sink. It was actually very nice.

The evening train left on schedule and headed for our first stop, Rome. Soon after we left I discovered that there was no restaurant car. This means there was no food on the train. This means no dinner.

Fortunately, we had had a good lunch in Amalfi, and we always carry water bottles of water. And I had bought a can of Coke before we left Positano and stuffed it in our bag.

In route to Rome, the train really moved. We tried to sleep, but it was difficult. Sleeping on a train can be tricky, even if you do have a bed, due to all the bouncing. We had just dozed off, or so it seemed, when we arrived in Rome. The Rome station is not a quiet station. There was all kinds of noise: people talking, announcements on the PA system, carts and train noises—in short, all kinds of ruckus.

After leaving Rome and throughout the night, the train speeds up, the train slows down. The train stops in stations, the train blows its whistle. There's all kinds of noise, you can't really sleep.

We're on the Wrong Train

I got up around 5:30 a.m. and, while headed for the bathroom, I asked the conductor what time we arrived in Venezia. He said six o'clock and gave me back our rail passes.

When I got back to our compartment, I got Shirley up so we could get ready and I could do things like shave in the little sink.

One item of note: In our compartment, under the sink, we found what we believe to be a chamber pot. After use, it looked as though when you put it back in its holder and closed the door, it dumped its contents onto the tracks below.

As the train was slowing I looked out the window and saw a sign that read *"Venezia Mestre"*: the same words that were printed on our reservation slip. This was not the main Venice train station. It was the second Venice station, on the mainland. Uh-oh.

Now the question was, "How do we get to the main Venice station, *Venezia Santa Lucia?*"

When I asked in my poor Italian, I was told to get off and go up alongside the train about nine or 10 cars. That part of the train was separating and was going on to Santa

Lucia. When we started our trip we were on the right train; now we were on the wrong train. While headed for the other part of the train we noticed our end (of the train) had indeed been disconnected. I soon found another train man, and a friendly one at that, and asked, *"Treno per Santa Lucia?"* (Is this the train to Santa Lucia?) and he said, *"Si."*

He also told us that it was only about a 10-minute ride across the lagoon and motioned us to get on with *"Prego."* (Please.).

By 6:30 in the morning we were in the *Venezia Santa Lucia* station, where food was our first priority.

In the train station's dining room, you find what you want to eat or drink, then tell the cashier. She gives you little chits of paper to give to the counterman, who in turn gives you what you want, in our case it was a cappuccino, a Coke and a couple of pastries. Delicious.

Even though we knew it would be impossible to get into our hotel this early, we still headed for it so we could dump our luggage before going out to explore Venice in the early morning. Our hotel, *La Fenice des le Artistes*, had supplied us with the information on how to get there from the train station.

We were to take *vaporetto* (waterbus) #1 or #82 from the *Piazza San Marco* and then walk from there. When I went to get vaporetto tickets I said, *"Per San Marco,"* and was told take boat #52. And, when we boarded the boat, I once again asked, *"Per San Marco?"* and the driver nodded. My thoughts were that it was highly unlikely that the *vaporetto* people were conspiring to get tourists on the wrong boat, so we got on.

Our route to San Marco was not through the Grand Canal but through the *Scomenzera* and *Guidecca* canals around the perimeter of Venice. It was probably faster.

We stepped off of the boat at the *S. Zaccaria* stop in front of the *Daneli Hotel*, which is adjacent to San Marco.

At this time of the morning, the canal front and the Piazza San Marco are virtually deserted—a sight few tourists have ever seen.

When we got to the hotel, the lobby was crowded, which seemed a bit odd, considering the hour. Nonetheless, we were able to leave our bags before setting out into Venice.

Red Is Not Always Right

On a cruise up the English Channel from Lisbon to Amsterdam, one of our ports of call was Le Palais, Belle Isle, a small island in the Bay of Biscay south of Brittany in France.

The island is roughly eight miles south of the town of Quiberon on the mainland of France and is about 11 miles long and six miles wide at its widest.

We arrived early in the day and anchored off the main village, Le Palais, in the fog.

I mention the fog for a reason. Looking towards shore, I could just make out the entrance to the harbor. The entrance to the harbor is fairly narrow, and on both sides of the entrance there is a wall with navigation lights atop small lighthouses. One light is red the other green, as one would expect. If you are coming into the harbor from the channel and you don't get the entrance correct, you crash your boat into a wall.

Herein lies the problem. Here in the US, anyone who boats has the mnemonic "red, right, returning" drilled into their head from early on. Meaning, as you head in towards shore or in a channel, you keep the red light or buoy on your right. Here in Le Palais however, the red was on the left, the port side, and the green light was on the starboard, or right. To me this was entirely wrong. If I was coming in to the harbor in a small boat in a heavy fog such as we had, I would run into the harbor wall. Not a good thing.

Perplexed, I went up to the ship's bridge where I found an officer who told me that "red, right, returning" does not apply in France. In fact, it is just the opposite. Well, crap. My thought was that Americans who come to this part of world and rent or buy a boat could be in big trouble. As it turns out, it is not just in France where "red, right, returning" does not work. It is that way in much of the world.

When I got home, I did some research. What I discovered was downright scary. Can you believe it wasn't until 1982 that the International Association of Marine

Aids to Navigation and Lighthouse Authorities (IALA) implemented the Maritime Buoyage System? Prior to this, there were more than 25 buoy systems in place around the world. Argh! This apparently caused numerous sinkings and deaths. It reminded me of my manufacturing background, where we often said, "The wonderful thing about standards is that there are so many to choose from."

The result of implementing the IALA standard is that now there are only two systems, A and B, and they are region-based.

In Region A, port or left is red and starboard or right is green. It includes Europe, Australia, New Zealand, parts of Africa, and most of Asia. When coming into a port or channel, the red light will be on the left.

In Region B, port or left is green and starboard or right is red. It includes North America, Central America, and South America—plus the Philippines, Japan and Korea. When coming into a port or channel the red light will be on the right. Or, "red, right, returning"

In conclusion, if you are from the western hemisphere, be aware that red is not always right. Be careful.

4. Food and Drink

There are times when traveling that you come across a meal that you will remember for the rest of your life. Hopefully for good reasons. In our travels there were many times, particularly with food, we found ourselves saying, "Well, this is not exactly what I expected."

Como Cappuccino

In the movie *A Month by the Lake*, the lake is Lake Como in northern Italy. The lake is also featured in *Casino Royale* and *Star Wars: Episode II Attack of the Clones*. At the south end of the lake is the town of Como.

Earlier, I mentioned that we were staying a few minutes north of town on the west side of the lake, at the *Villa Flori*. We had planned a day outing up the lake to visit Bellagio and Varenna. From our hotel we took a taxi into town, where we hoped to catch the lake boat north. At the ferry station there was schedule posted on the wall. It was indecipherable—even if I were fluent in Italian, which I am not. As there was a boat at the dock, I went to the ticket office, pointed to the boat and asked, *"Per Bellagio?"* (for/to Bellagio).

"Si," was the answer. So we bought round-trip tickets and got on board.

The trip up the lake took about two hours and we made several stops along the way. The weather varied dramatically; we started off in Como with hot sun, then it clouded up and got cool, then it started to rain. We were, after all at the base of the Alps.

By the time we got to Bellagio, about half way up the lake, it had cleared somewhat, and you could see that this was truly a sub-alpine lake; the mountains on either side went up thousands of feet. Along the shore were towns, villages and homes that were stunning—in particular, the *Villa del Balbianello*. This villa was used in *Star Wars: Episode II* and numerous other movies.

Disembarking in Bellagio, we decided food was a good idea and, after checking out the menus posted at several of the restaurants, we decided on the small cafe called the *Metropole* overlooking the water. We sat inside, as it was very cool.

As we were finishing lunch, we noticed one of the waiters was having a very difficult time dealing with a table of five ladies, German we think, who were using English to communicate with the waiter. They were trying to determine exactly how much each of them owed. Apparently, each had ordered different things, and with the *comperto* and the *servizo* (tip) included in the total bill, each had to figure her portion of the bill, *exactly*. It was inconceivable that anyone pay too much. I was pleased that they were not Americans.

After they left, we told the waiter that from our perspective, the ladies were crazy. And, unfortunately, we had seen this all too often in the United States, so it was not just a German or American thing.

After lunch, we strolled through the waterfront shops of Bellagio and hiked up to see the church. It was closed, with the sound of jackhammers coming from the interior. So it was probably good that we could not go in.

Back at the ferry dock we found a ticket person who spoke English, more or less, and he told us that the next boat to Como was at 3:50, almost two hours. I asked if we had time to go over to Varenna and he said, "Yes." In fact, we could catch the boat to Como from there, that is, if we bought a round trip ticket. We said, "Let's do it." This proved to be one of our better moves. Ever.

Varenna is one of the most beautiful towns on the lake; it was just what we expected of an Italian lake town. As we approached it on the ferry, the sun came out. Beautiful. Our exploration of the town took us past the *Hotel Olivedo*, which was where we were going to stay had we bought the train tickets to Varenna as originally planned.

We were pleased that we ended up in Como and the *Villa Flori* instead, it was more convenient. That said, Varenna has a promenade along the water, which gave us some great views of the town, the lake, and the surrounding mountains. It is a romantic destination.

Staying in Como actually worked out for the best. We were tired and if we had stayed in Varenna, we most likely would have had to change hotels again in order to get to the Milan airport on time for our departure.

Eventually we were back on the boat and headed south when I went to the bar in the dining area and said, *"Vorey il café con latte e Coke, per favore."* (I'd like coffee with milk, and a Coke, please.) The coffee I got was the best coffee I had ever had. It was orgasmic. It was like liquid tiramisu. I was hooked for life. Mrs. C. later told me that the look on my face told her that if she reached for my cup she would have suffered bodily harm.

Later that evening, back in Como, we took a taxi to the *Imbarcadero* restaurant at the *Hotel Metropole Suisse* in town for dinner. Our hotel had recommended this restaurant and gave us a card to give to the maître d' when we arrived. (The card had a secret message on the back, secret, because we couldn't read it: It was in Italian. Some nerve.)

We were treated as VIPs and dinner was exceptional. Recommendations are good, particularly if you get a card that introduces you as a preferred customer. Our last meal in Italy was a huge success.

Mussels in Dubrovnik

We had arrived in Dubrovnik, Croatia, by ship on a cruise in the Adriatic.

Dubrovnik is very a popular port and we were fortunate to be able to get into the town early before the big cruise ships arrived and began disgorging thousands of people into the city.

Our ship was quite small by comparison to some with over 2,000 passengers; we had only a couple hundred passengers. More important, we were the first ship to arrive on this particular day.

Dubrovnik is a walled city that is quite small and with its red tiled roofs it makes quite an impression.

We tendered ashore and as we stepped on the city quay, we could see other ships approaching. Soon the town would be overrun with thousands of tourists, but now Dubrovnik was just waking up.

A highlight of the city is walking the walls that surround it. As you walk the walls along the sea you notice that there are two different colors of roof tiles on the buildings. In the early 1990s during the war in Croatia, the majority of the town's roofs were damaged. You can tell the buildings that had damage by the difference in the color of the tiles. The newer tiles are brighter.

All in all, it took about eight years after the war for Dubrovnik to get the city back to its current state. It was very important to rebuild it as it had been because the whole town is a UNESCO World Heritage site. Obviously, being a UNESCO site did not prevent it from substantial damage. Today it is back to being a beautiful little city.

As lunchtime approached, we needed to cut through the city near the quay to get to a restaurant just outside the city walls, where we were to have a snack. This was an effort because now the area near the quay was almost impossible to get through due to the throngs of people. Not a good thing.

Eventually we get to our restaurant with our group of 12 intact and sat down beneath a huge spreading tree to a treat of local sparkling wine and cake. The view from our table looked back on the old city and its tiny harbor.

It was so lovely that we did not want to leave. We and another couple decided to stay at the restaurant for lunch. Mussels are the specialty of the area when they were in season, and they were in season. Three of our group ordered mussels, but I wanted the shrimp risotto that I had seen go by for another diner. We also asked our waiter to recommend a bottle of local wine. When our food arrived, all the mussels had been combined on one serving dish that was as long as the table was wide. *We had never seen such a mound of mussels.* It was all wonderful; I even got some. And there were mussels left over. "Wow" is the most appropriate word.

By the time we left the restaurant, one or two of the bigger ships were sailing away. Many of the people were gone. They had only been in port for a few hours. We had the whole day, meaning that we could explore more of the town on our own, which we did.

Lemoncello

We had taken the train from Rome to Naples, before heading further south for Sorrento. The ride to Naples took about three hours and was uneventful, probably because we had properly validated our rail passes.

When we arrived at the *Stazione Centrale* in Napoli, and loaded our bags onto a cart and headed into the station itself, a couple of men approached us asking if we were going to Sorrento and offered to help us with our bags. Inasmuch as I knew the reputation Naples has for rip-offs (cons and pickpockets) and because I knew where we were going, I declined.

The train for Sorrento, the *Circumvesuviana,* is just downstairs in the main station. Here I bought tickets for Sorrento then went down more stairs to the train platform itself. The trains south run every half hour or so and can be crowded at times. Our train was crowded, but at least we were able to sit. The trip to Sorrento has 14 stops and takes about an hour.

The end of the line for the *Circumvesuviana* is Sorrento, and upon exiting the train we got a taxi to our hotel, the *Parco dei Principi.* (A good idea since we didn't know where it was.) The *Parco* is set amid a gardens or park on a cliff overlooking the Bay of Naples. Here we had good news and bad news.

The good news was that they were expecting us; the bad news was we didn't like the room. The room had two twin beds, not what we wanted or expected. When we mentioned this, the reply was, "No problem, we'll push them together." This was marginally acceptable. The next problem was that there was no private balcony overlooking the sea. It just wasn't the room for us. I took a paper copy of our reservation and went down to the front desk to see what could be done; the paper stated exactly the type of room we had reserved. We moved into the room next door, one that did have a balcony and was an overall nicer room. The beds here, however, had to be moved together to create a matrimonial bed. I tipped the doorman and he remade the beds handsomely. I did not understand the separate beds. We were not in a 1950s television show where couples were not seen in the same bed together.

After we were situated in our room and because we hadn't had any lunch, we went down to the bar to see what we could find in the way of food.

The only food we were able to get was a ham and cheese sandwich (of sorts) on toast. We also ordered *lemoncello*, the local liquor that is made from lemons.

Shirley, being a fan of all things lemon, had read about it and was expecting to love it. She didn't. If fact, she hated it. I was expecting not to like it, but to my surprise, I thought it was delicious. I found it very refreshing. I have become a lifelong fan of *lemoncello*.

Shoes

It was just after 8 p.m. when we decided to go downstairs and have dinner at the hotel's restaurant. Dinner in Italy is usually at 8 o'clock or later. We were tired and really didn't feel like going out looking for food.

This is important: When you go out to dinner in Italy, where you are seated, and the thoughtfulness of your service, may very much depend on your shoes. The first thing the host or hostess does when they greet you is look at your shoes. Sometimes they are discreet, other times not so much. This was a case of not so much. If you have on leather shoes (not running or tennis shoes) you will get a much better table. And much better service.

The menu in the restaurant was not Italian but continental. In other words, it had large variety of non-Italian items. The hotel seemed to have a significant English and American clientele, which I suppose influences the menu. Our dinner was extraordinary. The veal with lemon entrees were excellent.

That evening we slept with the door to the balcony open so that we could hear the sea against the cliffs below. It was a noticeable improvement over the sounds of the streets of Rome.

We Have No Idea What We Ate

We were in Paris, and it was a Sunday morning. We had breakfast in our room because we wanted to get an early start to pick up a rental car and get out of town before traffic got too bad. I did not relish driving in Paris.

Ordinarily we would have taken the train out of Paris and picked up our rental car in a smaller city. The complication here was that the rental car offices in the cities near where we wanted to go (in Brittany) were closed on Sunday.

From out hotel, we took a taxi to the Montparnasse train station in Paris and then began looking for the AutoEurope/EuroCar office. I found Avis and National car rental within the train station. I tried to call AutoEurope but could not make a connection. Fortunately, when I asked a fellow traveler for help, he told me that when dialing within Paris you have to use "01" not just "1" to start the number.

Once I was able to connect with the EuroCar office, I learned that they were across the street, in the fourth level of a parking garage next to the Le Meridian hotel. They must get a great deal of walk-in business. From the time we arrived at Montparnasse to the time we were headed out of the parking garage was well over an hour. So much for beating the traffic.

Getting out of Paris was a trick and a half, as traffic was very heavy on the freeway. With some divine assistance we were able to find the route we wanted. It is probably a good thing that I did not notice my wife's white knuckle grip on the car door handle and center console.

Our destination for the day was Cancale, a small fishing town on the Atlantic coast near Mont St. Michelle.

Once we were away from the city and traveling on secondary roads, the driving was fairly easy. There are a great many roundabouts in lieu of traffic lights, so much so that there were probably fewer than five traffic lights between the time we got on the freeway in Paris and the time we got to St. Michelle. It was a beautiful day and driving through the country was a delight.

We arrived at Le Mont-Saint-Michelle, the cathedral that sits atop a small island a kilometer off the coast of Normandy, late in the afternoon. After a few quick photos we headed for our bed & breakfast, *Les Rimains* in Cancale. It took some effort but we finally got into the village of Cancale. We could not find any signs to lead us to our destination. I called them and was told that I needed to go behind the church. Once we did, there were signs.

The bed & breakfast (B&B) is a little six-room house that overlooks the sea from atop a high cliff. The room was small but had charm—an item sorely missing at our hotel in Paris.

Our dinner at *Relais Gourmand* was to be our most significant of the trip; and we knew it would be expensive. The restaurant, associated with the B&B and its sister hotel, is a gourmet restaurant and a regional showpiece. The B&B's owner, Olivier Roellinger, is a Michelin three-star chef. The restaurant sent a car that picked us up and took us to dinner. The restaurant was just as we had seen in the photographs on the web. It was lovely and we had a table overlooking the garden.

Our waiter spoke no English, and our French was not going to work for a gourmet dinner. That said, the dinner was essentially seafood and was exceptional. We did not know what we ate—except for the sea urchin.

We had a cheese course for desert that, to this day, has not been matched. It consisted of a variety of local cheeses that will never be exported and were simply heavenly.

When the bill came, it simply had our room name at the B&B on it, not our name or any other identifying characteristics.

The evening had been quite special. When we got back to our room, with no ambient light from nearby cities to pollute the sky, the stars were brilliant. We could see the lights of the distant coast, but could not make out Mont St. Michelle even though we knew it was there.

Our bill for dinner at the restaurant the night before was on our receipt when we checked out of the next morning. Not bad. We may have received a discount because we were guest at the B&B.

This Is Not What I Expected

We were in the South of France. Saying that you are staying in the South of France sounds very romantic. It is. We were staying in Nice, at the *Hôtel La Pérouse.* The hotel is small but nice; it sits across from the Mediterranean at the north end of the *Promenade des Anglais*, the Walk of the English, along the beach.

The morning clouds burned off fairly early and after a quick breakfast, we headed for the train station to try to catch the 10:18 to Cannes. It was mid-May, and we figured everyone would be headed to Monaco, for this was the day of the Grand Prix. In fact, when we got to the train station, there was a man with a sign in front of the station reading "Need a Grand Prix ticket." Yes, in English.

We made it to the station in time to get tickets and catch the train south. The marquee said that the express train to Cannes was running 10 minutes late. On the platform there were two trains. Both said, "Cannes." As we got on one, the other closed its doors and left. It turned out the other train was the *express* and this was the local, which would take a few minutes longer to get to our destination. No worries.

When we got to Cannes, we got off and walked towards the waterfront. We realized rather quickly that not everyone had gone to the Grand Prix. We were in the middle of the Cannes Film Festival. It is an extraordinary experience. There were large numbers of people, and many were in costumes or made up in some manner promoting the latest movie. It is difficult to describe, except that there were an extraordinary number of exotic cars and exotic ladies, perhaps more than in Monaco.

When we got hungry, we opted for lunch on the beach at the restaurant of the *Hotel Martinez*. The weather was gorgeous, the sun was out, and the light on the bay sparkled. We were seated under an umbrella and given menus.

On the menu I saw that they had one of my favorites, a *tagliatelle carbonara*, like a *fettuccine carbonara* only with different pasta. I'd have that.

When my *carbonara* came, there was an egg yolk on top of it. This is not exactly what I expected. Fortunately, I knew that the egg was to be mixed in with the pasta and sauce. Shirley had ordered a salad *Niçoise*. Even though it was not what I expected, lunch was excellent.

That evening in Nice, around eight o'clock, we walked to the nearby plaza that in the daytime had been the flower market. In the evening, the restaurants spill out into the plaza. We had dinner at *Le Grand Bleu*—a place that specialized in seafood. We shared a salad and a small bottle of the house wine. It was so good we should have ordered a full bottle.

Shortly after we sat down, a gentleman near us from England spoke to us because we were the first English speaking voices he had heard in three days. He had come over for the Grand Prix by himself (his wife was not interested in racing). I told him I was amazed he could hear at all because the cars are so loud.

Another young English-speaking couple then sat between the man from England and us. We helped them with their menus, so I'm sure the man from England got a good deal of his native tongue—though Americanized.

What Language Do I Speak?

We see ourselves fortunate as Americans that English is such a common language. So much so that it is said if a Frenchman and a Norwegian meet somewhere in the world, they will be able to converse in English.

Most times when we travel we try to limit ourselves to one, or at the most two, countries. The key reason for this is so that we only have to deal with one or two foreign languages.

One trip in particular we completely blew this objective. We had started out in Spain, where we did okay with our Spanish. Then we boarded a cruise in Barcelona. It took us to ports in France, Italy and back to France before returning to Barcelona.

From Barcelona we flew to Nice on the French coast. (We flew because the train schedules were not convenient.) As our trip included so many countries, we had used Spanish, Italian, French, and of course English. I don't want to give the impression that I speak all these languages. I do not, not even close. I do, however, generally try to use the local language when I can, such as when ordering dinner.

When we went out for dinner our first night in Nice, I attempted to order dinner in French. Big mistake. In one sentence I used four different languages. My brain was a jumble of languages. The waiter looked at me strangely. (I am being kind here.) I finally ordered in English. This was the only language in which I could put together a coherent sentence.

We got a big laugh out of this, as did some of the people at a nearby table. The waiter probably did not.

No Menu

As I noted earlier, we have frequently find ourselves saying, "This is not exactly what I expected." I seemed to find myself saying this repeatedly during travels in Italy. Much of the time, these were the first words out of my mouth once my dinner was placed before me. Fortunately, what usually followed next was, "I like it."

It was in the Tuscany region, near Florence, that Mrs. C. and I had some of our more interesting dining experiences. Though the word "dining" does not seem to have the right connotation. It implies, at least to me, something slightly formal; it implies menus. Menus are something you don't always find in the restaurants of Tuscany.

It was our first night in Prato, more accurately in the hills above Prato, at the *Villa Rucellai Frattoria di Canto*. Our instructions on getting to the villa were a little vague; once we exited the *autostrada* at Prato we were to essentially follow the signs to the restaurant "*La Fontana*," and the villa would be a little past that. There were a lot of "La Fontana" signs.

The *Villa Rucellai* is a 16th-century farmhouse/villa that does not have a restaurant, but its owners Giovanna and Paolo Piqué, were pleased to recommend several places where we might find something delicious to eat. The obvious first choice was "*La Fontana*," basically because we knew where it was or at least the signs. Paolo called for reservations, but we couldn't get in due to rain. It seems that most of the seating at "*La Fontana*" is on an outside terrace, and with the rain, everyone who had reservations was going to have to squeeze inside, where the seating is very limited. Paolo suggested we try *Logi's* instead. It too was nearby.

Being very hungry travelers, we headed out for the restaurant around 7 o'clock, but finding the restaurant was not as easy to find as Paolo had led us to believe. We parked in front of an old stone church, as we had been instructed, and started to walk up the hill, but where was the restaurant? We found a house with a sign on it, but the sign didn't say "*Logi's.*" We decided to ask. This was indeed the place, however they didn't open till eight. Ok. Instead of waiting around for them to open, we drove into Prato to explore the city. When we re-arrived there was only one other customer there. We hoped this was because most Italians don't eat until 8:30 or 9:00. It was. By nine the place was packed.

After being seated, our waiter asked what language we wished to speak, a novel concept. We opted for English.

He told us about their local wine, and we said we'd try it. The wine arrived in a bottle with no label. We knew it was indeed local. It was excellent. Our waiter then proceeded to tell us about the antipasto (I love the sound of that word, "anti-pasto"), which sounded very interesting, so we decided to give it a try as well. The antipasto was extraordinary, a collection of local meats, salamis and such, and *crostini. Crostini* are little slices of toasted baguettes that are topped with an assortment of toppings. One of ours was a Tuscan paté that was earthy, slightly bitter, but very tasty.

It was only when our waiter began to describe the pasta dishes that we realized there was no menu. "Uh-oh," We had no idea how much anything was. I asked how much they were, "*Questa pranzo?*" He told us and it was about par for pasta dishes, so we thought, "Why worry?

Let's just go for it." Mrs. C. had pasta with *porcini* mushrooms, and I had pasta with meat sauce flavored with duck. It was not exactly what I expected, but it was, like the antipasto, extraordinary!

Unfortunately, the pasta dishes filled us up, so we had to bypass the main course. Next time we'll share the pasta. We did, however, save room to share tiramisu for dessert. Everything about the dinner was truly Tuscan: the food, the atmosphere, and the people. This was, indeed, a marvelous place to eat. The total bill came to about 30 dollars US.

When we got back to the villa after our dinner, we were able to get in to the building, but there were no light switches, at least not any that we could find. And no one was around. I know this because we could not be quiet finding our way back up the stairs to our room in the dark. I guess back in the days of the Medicis, people carried flash-candles.

At the *Villa Rucellai*, a breakfast is served in the great dining room. The room is huge and has a large table that is the same dark rich color of the floor. Unlike the floor, the table doesn't creak. There was juice, coffee, cereal, yogurt and other assorted breakfast items set out for the guests to enjoy as desired. The toaster was like no other toaster I have ever seen. It was either an antique or an advanced Italian design. It took a bit of time to figure it out. The coffee was exceptionally good, but very strong. The different types of coffee are one of the hidden delights in European travel. I have very fond memories of this particular villa, with its garden and view overlooking Prato.

5. France

We have been to France several times, and each time it always turns out to interesting, often it becomes an adventure—whether we were watching shop keepers attempting to put up an awning in Paris or being confounded by a truckers' strike.

The Knife

We had rented a car in Reims, about 140 kilometers northeast of Paris. Our thinking was that getting the car outside of Paris would be preferable to driving in Paris traffic.

When we arrived in Reims, it was just after noon, so the rental car agency was closed for lunch. They take long lunches in France, so we were not going to be able to get the car until after two o'clock. We might as well do as the Romans, or in this case, the French do, and have a long leisurely lunch, ourselves.

When we eventually got the car and headed out of town, we took the road less traveled towards Épernay in the heart of the Champagne region. When we got into town, we checked in with the tourist office to see what they could recommend for a place to spend the night.

The place we selected was a little bed & breakfast a few kilometers out of town. When we got there, we found it to be a small château complete with a moat. Our room was on the second floor and was connected to the dining room below via a stone spiral staircase. I suppose this was so that the lord of the manor was able to sneak down to the kitchen at night for a snack.

What we had not anticipated in making our selection on where to stay was food. Oops. The château had no restaurant and we were not able to discern if there was something nearby. We wanted something simple, which to us Americans means something like a sandwich or a pizza. Good luck finding this in rural France.

I set out to see what I could find. A couple of kilometers from the château I saw what looked to be a small village off in the distance on a side road off to my left. As I turned on to the road magic happed. It was dusk, and I felt as if I had just driven into a Van Gogh painting.

It was in the late afternoon sun on the fields made them glow gold. It was absolutely breathtaking.

But I was hungry. I drove through the village I had seen hoping to find a place that looked like it might sell food, but did not see anything. After passing through, I thought that I had seen a bar. They might have food. I doubled back, parked the car and went in.

It was a small local place and I asked if I could get a couple of sandwiches. They said, *"Oui,"* and I knew I was in luck. From my perspective, all sandwiches in France are made with *jambon* (ham). I was asked if I wanted my sandwiches "*avec salad?*"

"*Oui, avec salad and mayonnaise.*" I said, meaning Yes, with lettuce and tomato. I also got a couple of Cokes to go. Yes, the sandwiches were on baguettes. This was French fast food after all. Perfect.

I took them back to Mrs. C. at the *château*. We ate them sitting on our bed. They were wonderful.

The next morning we had continental breakfast in the *château* dining room before heading back into Épernay to visit the champagne houses. In France it is okay to drink champagne at any time of the day. It is here in the US too, but it seems more appropriate in France.

The main street in Épernay is the Champagnes Avenue where the main champagne producers of the area have tasting rooms. Here you'll find the likes of *Pierre-Joulët, Mercier, Pol Roger*, and of course, *Moët et Chandon*. All have tastings after the tours. The tours take you deep into the underground wine cellars that extend for miles underneath the town. I wonder how they don't run into each other. I think we enjoyed *Moët et Chandon* the most, and to this day, Shirley thinks we should have had some shipped home.

After lunch we headed towards the town of Nancy (pronounced non-cy). After a while we came into a small town and the traffic, what there was of it, just stopped. There were tractors and trucks blocking the road. We sat there for a while wondering what the problem was, when the car in front of us backed up and then went through a parking lot and then headed down a side road to circumvent the blockage. We followed him, thinking we'd get around the problem, and we did.

We didn't think too much about what we had encountered until the next day when, as we came into a small town around lunchtime, we found several semi-trucks blocking the road. I said to Shirley, "Something is obviously going on that we don't know about."

We'd been sitting there for a few minutes when a woman a couple of cars in front of us that was full of kids got out of her car and went around to her hatch-back, opened it, and came out with a knife. A very large chef's knife. She went up to the men standing around the trucks and began threatening them with it—in their face. Saying she was angry is an understatement.

After a bit of discussion they agreed to let her pass and moved one of the trucks. She took off, as did the car in front of us and as did we. When the truck moved, we zipped on by. We went through parking lots and down one-way streets the wrong way, just following the car in front of us. It worked; we made it past the blockade.

We learned later that it was a French truckers' strike. The French seem to strike a lot. To make their point, they'd block the roads for an hour or so in the afternoons. It seems that they were protesting that their licenses would be marked with points if they were involved in an accident. And after accumulating x number of points, their licenses would be suspended for a time.

We will always remember the lady with the knife.

These Horses Have a Problem

On another occasion we were driving in France's Loire Valley, the château country about 150 miles south of Paris. The valley is along the middle stretch of the Loire River and it is a gorgeous area of France. A special treat would be to take a hot air balloon ride over the region either in the early morning or late in the afternoon.

We were staying at the *Château La Bourdaisière*, a 19th-century county house in the Commune of *Montlouis-sur-Loire*. From there it is about an hour's drive to the *Château of Chambord*, one of the largest and most renowned of the *château* in this part of France.

Chambord has, as one of its claims to fame, an interior staircase designed by Leonardo da Vinci that is two intertwined staircases that never meet, a helix of sorts. People going up might never meet those going down. In a time of kingly assignations, this could be a good thing.

We arrived in mid-afternoon and had hoped to see a horse show at 4 o'clock. Apparently this was not held on the day we were there. Figures.

There was a shop that sold locally produced food items, and we bought some fresh goat cheese and duck/goose rillettes (a form of pate) sealed in a glass jar for a picnic dinner back at our château.

As we were going through the town of Pontloy on our way back to La Bourdaisière, we made a wrong turn, and by the time we got back on the right road we found what looked and smelled like horse manure on the road. Had there been a parade?

As we went on, there was more and more of it. There was horse shit all over the road. We thought these horses have a real problem. You can imagine the smell.

Then there was more! And it did not let up. In fact, it was getting worse. How was this possible?

We eventually caught up to a tractor pulling a load of horse manure and it was falling out of the bottom. We got around him as quickly as possible.

By the time we got back to *La Bourdaisière*, it was pretty much time to eat, so I managed to get some French bread (a baguette) from our hosts and a couple of Cokes from a shop across the courtyard, and we ate in our room. This sounds easy but it was not. We had a quite a time getting into the *rillettes*; we couldn't get the jar open. Well, crap. We tried hot water and everything we could think of before sneaking down to the kitchen to find something to help us pry the lid off. Yes, the *rillettes* were very good.

Haven't They Done This Before?

We were staying in a small hotel on the left bank of the Seine in Paris. This allowed the ability to do one of the most enjoyable things in Paris, to find a small café for breakfast. Breakfast is usually simple, a café (coffee) or a hot chocolate and a croissant. There is a place we like on the Rue de Seine where I had my first true French *cafe au lait* (coffee with milk) many years ago. The cafes of Paris are somehow unique. They have a distinctive aroma and taste that is just not matched in the states. A coffee in a French Café is not the same as Starbucks. Shirley has similar feelings about her *chocolate chaud* (hot chocolate); here it's dark, thick and bitter—and definitely not made from a mix.

On one particular morning as we sat in the café with our coffee and chocolate, we began watching the proprietors of a shop across the street, putting up a canopy in front of their shop. It was similar to one of those canopies you see at farmers markets or art shows to cover the wares of the vendors.

They put the canopy up. They took it down. They put it up, they took it down. They turned it 90°, and then they put it up, and then took it down again. Hadn't they done this before? Like every day? Each time they put it up, it looked the same to us. Eventually, after four or five times, they seemed satisfied. Or perhaps they just gave up.

Are We Dead?

Museums are a big thing to us. Where we go is sometimes dictated by museums we want to visit or revisit. In fact, the Pergamon Museum is the real reason we wanted to visit Berlin. In Paris, the biggest museums and the most popular are the Louvre and the D'Orsay. Our favorite is the D'Orsay, probably because it is smaller and more manageable than the Louvre and because it has more impressionist paintings that we like.

The Louvre is huge, and it can take days to see it all, if you can. It will wear you out. It is also much more crowded, particularly with school field trips. I can't say I understand this part; I just can't see school children ages eight to 12, or younger, really caring about art at all.

It might have been our first trip to Paris, and we were at the Louvre. It was lunchtime, and we needed a break. Fortunately there is a cafeteria of fair size in the Louvre underneath the glass pyramid that is the main entrance.

We had retrieved our lunch and sat down when shortly thereafter we heard angels singing. Had a bomb gone off? Were we dead?

I asked Shirley if she heard the singing and she said, "Yes."

I checked myself and all my parts seemed to be there; I saw no destruction near us. Looking around, nothing was out order. From where was the music coming? Certainly not the PA system. It was too clear and beautiful. I went to search for the source. I found it. Just outside the entrance to the cafeteria the Vienna Boys Choir was singing. In an impromptu concert. What voices! We were not dead.

6. Italy

There is so much I could write about Italy. It is fabulous. The food is wonderful, and I particularly enjoy the wine. My best bit of advice about dining in Italy is to always order the house wine, the *vino de casa*. Red or white (*rosso* or *bianco*), it doesn't matter, it will be good. The restaurant only serves what they are proud of. You will be pleased.

How do you find a good restaurant or *trattoria*? Look for local customers, not tourists, and harried, busy waiters.

Let's talk about red buttons for a minute, particularly in Italy. My opinion is that if you are in Italy and you are in a situation where you don't know what to do and there is a red button in front of you, push it. I'll explain. . .

On the Lido

Many cruise ships have *Lido* decks. Presumably they get their name from the town or island of Lido, which is just a short boat ride from Venice. Lido is described as a fashionable resort town on the Adriatic that is dedicated primarily to shopping and bathing, as it has many beaches where people go to swim. It is far less crowded than Venice, and there are no canals.

For most tourists, the islands of Murano, Burano, and Torcello are the top three-day trips from Venice. Having seen those, we wanted something different, and the island of Lido was it. There is more than one *vaporetto* (water bus) line that goes from Venice out to the Lido so when you go, you choose the one that best meets your needs.

Once when we were on Lido, not too far from the ferry dock, I felt nature calling. Along the street was an automated public toilet. They self-clean and sanitize after each use. It costs 1 euro to use them. I deposited my coin and a panel opened and I stepped inside. Inside was a very modern inside, there was a sink a toilet, and a lot of whooshing noises.

I proceeded to take care of business, but then, I did not see how I was supposed to get out. There was nothing indicating how to exit. There were no signs either. I called to my wife outside and said, "You may have to put another euro in the slot if I can't figure out how to get out."

There was, however, a *very* big red button. When all else fails, push the red button. I did, and the door opened.

Getting There From Here

Once you arrive at your primary destination city, assuming you are coming in by air, train, or some means other than driving, you have to get into town, or wherever you are staying. How do you get there from here? On my first several trips to Europe this was of great concern to me. It can be even more of a concern when going to a country where you do not speak the language.

If you have not made arrangements for someone to meet you, you are on your own once you arrive at your destination airport or train station. If you are going on a cruise and going to the ship directly from the airport, there is usually a cruise line agent there to meet you. Even if you have made arrangements for someone to meet you, what do you do if they aren't there? This happens. Sometimes you are just on your own and you need to handle it.

On one trip we were headed for Padova, Italy. It's in the Venato region on the mainland, a little more than 20 miles from Venice. You cannot fly into it. From the US we were connected in Amsterdam, where our itinerary called for us to change planes for our flight to Venice. A simple task, not necessarily so? At Schiphol, the Amsterdam airport, the overhead reader boards that show departing flights seemed a bit scarce. What they do have, however, are devices that scan your ticket/boarding pass bar code and then tell you the gate for your next flight. I do not see this as an improvement as there can be queues.

In our case it was a good 15-minute walk to our departure gate, time that did not include going through the Schiphol Immigration booth and the security re-check. Interestingly, most times they do not ask if you are traveling on business or for pleasure like they used to. I assume they don't care.

In route to our connecting gate way we stopped at a cash machine, a bank-o-mat in European terms, to get some money, in this case euros. Our bank/debit cards worked. Nice. One never knows. (A reminder: Today it is highly advisable to let your bank know that you will be traveling overseas and to which countries, if you want your bank card to work.)

I will digress here for a moment. We were in Positano, Italy and we needed to get some cash. While the ATMs were not that hard to find, the question was whether or not they would give us money. The first couple of machines I tried to use apparently did not like my debit card and refused my request. I probably cursed at the machine. Crossing the street and using another ATM, I had no problem. It seems that the first machine was from a German bank, and I was in Italy. The Italian cash machines liked my debit card. I said *grazie* (thank you) to the machine. So, the advice to be gleaned from this story is: Don't attempt to use German bank-based ATMs unless you are in Germany. (We've had trouble with German bank ATMs on more than one occasion.) If at all possible use only ATMs from banks in the country you are visiting.

Back to Schiphol. Eventually I will get to the point. While waiting for our flight to Venice, I watched the people. Fascinating. Across from us was a lady who was far too tan. She was wearing a ring with what looked like a Chinese pagoda on it. It could easily cause bodily damage, like putting someone's eye out. She had enough metal jewelry on her to build a small car. I am glad we weren't behind her in the security line.

The metal lady was the *entertaining* part of waiting for our next flight. The *annoying* part was the voice for the moving walkway behind us saying over and over and over: "Walkway ending, watch your step." The recording was in English. We were in The Netherlands. Are English-speaking people the only ones who do not notice the automated walkway is ending? Perhaps the recording would be better if it gave you more useful information, such as, "If you're an American, don't try to use German ATMs in Italy."

When we arrived at the Marco Polo airport outside of Venice, we retrieved our luggage and went outside to find transportation to Padova. Cesar, at our hotel in Padova, had told us via email that we could take the *Sita* bus to Padova. (Padova and Padua are the same city.) As he had said, when we exited the airport, the bus was right there.

I said to the driver, *"Por Padova,"* (for Padova) and he said, *"Si."* Do I speak Italian well or what? The price for the two of us was 10€.

As we set off on the bus, I noticed that all the signs I was seeing did not say Padova, they say "Venice". Then we were driving across the causeway to Venice. As it turned out, Venice was just a stop. I presumed we were on the right bus. After dropping off a few passengers and picking up a few, we headed back across the causeway and on to a freeway where we rode for what seemed like quite a distance. By watching the signs, it did indeed look like we were headed for the city of Padova. This was good news. Our next question was, "Where do we get off?" This became obvious when we got to the bus station in Padova and everyone got off. From there we took a cab to our hotel.

When we pulled up in front of the hotel, a young man came outside and said, "You must be Mr. Chesnutt." I replied, "Yes," figuring it was in our best interest to tell the truth. From the time we got on the bus at the Venice airport until we arrived at the hotel was just a little over an hour. Not bad.

Cesar at the front desk apparently had many things he wanted to tell us, things about the city and things we could do and where to eat. This was not a good idea. I told him that anything he told us we would not remember; our minds were too tired for anything he might say to be remembered. Disappointed, he showed us to our room— which was very nice, modern Italian, just like the picture on the hotel's website, and it looked out onto the Basilica of St. Anthony across the street. We rested with our eyes closed.

Lost Things

In Padova, the Basilica of St. Anthony is obviously dedicated to St. Anthony. He is the Saint of Lost Things. I do not understand how this was established, nonetheless people pray to him to help them find lost things. And, according to the letters posted in the Basilica, many people have found what they were looking for after asking for St. Anthony's help.

The Basilica also contains a gold reliquary that contains the chin and tongue of the Saint. This to me brings to mind a plethora of questions, least of which is: where is the rest of Saint Anthony? Why do they only have the chin and tongue and wouldn't the tongue have completely decomposed by now? It seems that a few centuries ago if you were someone of note, when you died they sent parts of your body to various different places. Richard the Lionheart's heart for example is in the cathedral in Rouen. I think it was a prestige thing.

The Gucci Store

When we were staying outside of Florence in Prato we took several daily excursions. One such excursion was to Siena, about 40 miles south of Florence. Cars are not allowed in the old section of Siena—probably a good idea—where things haven't changed much in the past 300 years, at least architecturally. When we arrived, there were intermittent rain squalls and the city was surrounded by dark storm clouds that only seemed to add to the renaissance feeling. We walked the cool, wet streets, marveling at the colors and shapes of the centuries-old buildings. Siena seems to bring out the romance in your soul.

Lunch in Siena was at a little place on the corner of the cobbled Piazza del Campo. While sipping some wine and waiting for our order to arrive, it began to rain. In an instant the waiters rolled out an awning to cover us, and we watched the people in the piazza scramble for cover. As we ate our crostini and pizza, we found it difficult to imagine the *Palio*, the anything goes, and usually does, horse race that is run on the piazza twice a year. You could get killed in the *Palio*. So could your horse, and from the looks of the piazza, so could the spectators.

Leaving Siena, we headed for San Gimignano, a 13th-century walled city to the northwest of Siena. San Gimignano is much smaller than Siena and has 13 medieval towers overlooking the surrounding green, rolling hills of the Tuscan countryside. Oddly, at least to us, San Gimignano seemed to have more tourists than Siena and it also seemed to lack some of the charm as well; it could have been the tourists that caused this. In any case, I suppose, it is a matter of personal taste. On the other hand, San Gimignano does have some truly wonderful boar salami, made from the wild boar found in the surrounding hills. This was Shirley's first taste of boar.

On the way back to Prato, I did not want to use the major freeways. I wanted to use the more picturesque back roads. This was in the days before GPS so all we had was a map. I was following the minor road headed north, going through small towns. At one point we felt like we were in one continuous small town. Then as we passed one street, I saw a Gucci store. Small towns don't have Gucci stores. Somehow we had accidently ended up in Florence. This was confirmed as we drove across a river that turned out to be the Arno River. I was able to deduce this because I saw the *Ponte Vecchio* (bridge) over the river a few hundred yards away. Brilliant. The good news was that I knew how to get to Prato from here. And I knew about the red button on the motorway.

Where are the Women

We were a bit late getting back to the *Villa Rucellai*, so after we cleaned up a bit we rushed off to *Logi's*, hoping they would remember us and let us in. When we got there, it was almost full, but we managed to catch the eye of our waiter from the night before and he found us a table, the last one. Dinner that evening consisted of wine, *insalata mista* (mixed salad), *penne puttanesca, ribellitto*—a thick twice-cooked Tuscan soup made from cannellini beans—and a lime-grilled quarter chicken as the main course. And of course, dessert. Once again, it was absolutely super.

Mrs. C. made the observation during dinner that most of the people at the tables in the restaurant were men; many in large groups. Where were the women? Did they stay home or go to different restaurants?

Dining out in Italy

A couple of notes on eating out in Italy: Several years ago, on a trip to Rome, I learned that it is hard to go wrong ordering the house wine in Italy. To Italians it is something that represents their restaurant, something they take pride in and it is usually very good. It is not simply a "cheaper" wine, like what we might find as the house wine here in the US. Most house wine come in a carafe, which is usually a liter. It is possible to order a mezzo *litro* of wine, which is a half-liter.

Second, most Italians eat later in the evening, around 8:30 or 9:00 o'clock. As a result, you won't have the feeling of being rushed, the table is generally yours for the evening, and they don't have the table turnover like we do here in America. There, the table is yours for the evening.

One thing we noticed during the course of our travels was that Italy doesn't seem to have very many overweight people; in fact we could probably count the number of truly *large* Italians we saw on one hand. Perhaps it's their lack of fast food, or perhaps it's the red wine. All I know is they generally seem a lot fitter than Americans. Mrs. C. says she is considering going on a pasta diet.

By law, restaurants in Italy must be closed at least 1½ days a week. Most are closed for two. We also learned that "the criteria" for finding a good restaurant is to look for: tablecloths, flowers, local people eating there, and busy waiters. This criteria found us the perfect place for lunch in Piza, Venice and Verona.

If you are fortunate enough to visit Tuscany, take some chances when you eat out. Try some of the local specialties. Expect the unexpected and the beef to be rare. And, give the rabbit a try. Hopefully, you, as I, will find yourself saying, "I love it".

For an afternoon treat, try the *riso gelato* (rice), a local favorite. It has a very clean taste and provided a much-needed pick-me-up.

For us tiramisu is the desert of choice in Italy; it may be similar where ever you try it, but it will always be different and never quite the same.

A Dinner to Remember

Discoveries of all kinds await the traveler in Venice. Memorable discoveries can be found along a quiet canal or sometimes in a noisy *trattoria* on a street that caters to tourists. In some cases, your discoveries may be serendipitous and for you alone, or they may be for the population in general. Speaking for myself, some of the best discoveries of Venice were made sitting at a table with people placing food in front of me. As I have mentioned, there were times when you find yourself saying, "This is not exactly what I expected" and times when you say, "I am in heaven." In many cases, the phrases were uttered back to back.

One such occasion I remember in particular was in Venice. We had arrived by train in the early evening and Mrs. C. and I had two things on our minds: first, to find our hotel; and second, to find food. The first was accomplished easily as our hotel was fairly near the train station in the Cannaregio district. The second was a little more involved. As most Italian restaurants don't really open till 7:30 or 8:00, we had some time to wander the streets along the Grand Canal before dinner. Sergio at the desk in our hotel said we couldn't get too lost. I think he lied. The only way we were able to find our way back was by following signs that read "Ferrovia," where the train station was located.

The place we found for dinner pretty much fit the bill. The waiters were not exceptionally busy, but in all other areas, the criterion was met. The restaurant, the *Trattoria Vittoria* on *St. Geremia*, turned out to be absolutely marvelous. We elected to bypass the *"Turista"* menu and ordered a la carte, an excellent move. We started out with a liter of the house white wine using our somewhat limited language skills *"Uno litero di vino bianco du casa, per favore."* (A liter of the house white wine, please.)

The wine, which came in a liter carafe, was excellent—by far the best we had in Italy. We each had an *insalata mista* or mixed salad, and to our surprise there were no shredded carrots on it. This was a good thing; we were tiring of carrots on anything that even slightly resembled a salad. We each selected one of the pasta dishes as our main course; spaghetti with clams for Mrs. C. and spaghetti marinara for me. Both were excellent.

When dinner was done, I turned to notice the cook in the kitchen watching us—I'm sure she was someone's *nonna* (grandmother). I smiled and said, *"Perfetto,"* perfect. She replied with a nod and a beaming smile.

Dinner was the good news; the bad news was that Mrs. C. wanted to shop on the way back to our room. Normally this would not be an issue, but the wine had been so good that I had drank a great deal of it. And there was no one to take me back to the room on a hand truck.

San Marco Entertainment

The piazza San Marco in Venice is quite large. In the mid-afternoon the piazza or square is always entertaining. You can sit with a glass of wine or a coffee and watch the tourists and pigeons playing with each other-. At times it seems as if it is some sort of bizarre contest between the tourist and the pigeons.

You can get a gelato and sit on a stoop, or you can take a table at one of the cafes on either side of the piazza. On one particular day we elected to have an afternoon gelato and listen to the musicians at the restaurants lining the square play music of Mozart and Elton John; it was wonderful. (I noted that the different bands took turns and did not play at the same time.)

If you are on the piazza when peaches are in season and you see a Bellini on the menu, have it. There is no place better.

As you probably know every year in February, the Venetians celebrate Carnival. There are elaborate parties and balls with elaborate costumes and masks. The diversity of the masks is incredible, ranging from the simple to the macabre and grotesque. Not all the mask shops are geared for tourist, some are quite remarkable. While you may not be a character in the movie "Amadeus," you may nonetheless find the mask that is you, or your avatar. A favorite souvenir of Mrs. C. is a mask she found at a local shop that makes them in house.

Gondolas

When we were staying in the Cannaregio area we asked Sergio, the desk clerk at our hotel who was friendly and knew the answers to the key questions that we tourists ask, where was the best place to get a gondola ride?

Sergio's answer was, "Near the piazza San Marco, near Harry's bar."

It seemed a slightly surprising answer since you can find gondolas almost everywhere and Harry's Bar was quite a ways down the Grand Canal. None the less we took his advice.

A few years back, Harry's was the local hangout of a writer named Hemingway. Not surprisingly, Harry's was the haunt of Colonel Richard Cantwell in the novel *Across the River and Into the Trees*, a love story of sorts that takes place in Venice just after WWII. I don't think the book is all that well known, but I like it.

Around 7 o'clock we took the *vaporetto* to the *piazza San Marco*. From there, we doubled back along the Grand Canal and found the gondola station at the *S. Marco Vallaresso* near Harry's. I asked how much it would be and the price was about par so we climbed aboard.

Our ride through the canals was absolutely wonderful and this was the time of day to do it. We explored the little canals as well as the *Grand* one. Along the way, we noticed the local young ladies along the way seemed to be "eyeing" our gondolier. We believe he "eyed" them back. Even though our gondolier spoke very little English, he pointed out several sites we never would have known were there, including the houses of Mozart and Goethe and the Ducal residence. The gondola and boat traffic jams we encountered in the tiny canals only added to the ride. At one point, we encountered a boat of musical troubadours whose music and song was what you only dream of hearing on the canals on Venice. Our ride only heightens our memories of Venice. We must be true romantics.

We returned to the *Trattoria Vittoria* for dinner, a place where we had had dinner before. We returned to test the theory that if you visit a restaurant once, you're just a customer; twice, you're a friend; and three times, you're a regular. Mrs. C. would say we returned for the wine. I think her opinion is closer to the truth. Once again the dinner was first rate.

7. Russia

Although we did not see much of Russia, only St. Petersburg, we found it fascinating and well worth visiting. We were on a cruise of the Baltic and St. Petersburg was one of our ports-of-call.

This is another short chapter; it relates our experiences, observations and things we were told by our tour guides.

White Nights

It was June as we were headed into Neva Bay from the Baltic towards St. Petersburg. I was awake at 2:15 in the morning, and opening the curtains and looking out, I could see that our sunset was turning into sunrise; this far north it is hard to tell the difference, but either way there is enough light to read outdoors, even at this hour. These nights are said to be white nights.

Prior to our arrival in St. Petersburg Mrs. C. attended a seminar about shopping in Russia, what to buy and where. She learned that there was an on-board Russian Bazaar. She also learned the perils of shopping on-shore where items for sale could be of questionable quality. There have been cases where people bought what they thought was caviar and it turned out when they got it home to be black shoe polish. In other cases, jewelry claimed to be amber turned out to be plastic. The warning may have been a marketing ploy, but we will never know.

For these reasons above and because our access to shopping in St. Petersburg would be limited, if any at all, Mrs. C. and I agreed that our purchases of Russian items would be made on the ship.

I found it quite interesting that if we were to go on excursions other than those arranged by the cruise line, we would need visas. These visas can take up to six months to obtain and cost around $200. With excursions from our ship, we are given temporary visas that we would give back at the end of the day. Also, unlike other countries' currencies, the ship's bank could not sell us Russian rubles. You might think that this would be a problem. Not so. From what we heard, one can use just about any currency in your pocket to purchase goods in St. Petersburg, dollars in particular.

There also seemed to be a great deal of restrictions, not so much about what we, as tourists, could and could not do, but more about what tour operators or personal drivers could and could not do. It sounds as if Russian bureaucracy has not relinquished much of its control since the fall of communism. We would see.

As we came into the port, the day was clear and the temperature in the sixties. St. Petersburg is the largest port in Russia, something that I could easily see from the upper deck of our ship. I also noted two other large cruise ships following us into the docks. I would hate to be a non-cruise ship tourist, or local trying to get into any of the cities tourist sites today, there would be just too many people.

Ashore in St. Petersburg

As we disembarked we were met on shore by a small band. No problem there. The problem was, somewhat disconcertingly, they were playing American songs. I am in Russia—I want Russian music. Why would they think we would want to hear Beatles or Lionel Richie music? This happens in many countries more often than you would think.

When we disembarked the ship, we proceeded through Russian customs, where they stamped our passports and gave us our temporary visas. Then, after boarding our coach, we were off.

We had a short tour of the city before being unloaded in front of the Hermitage. The Hermitage Museum was formerly the palace of Catherine the Great and other Russian monarchs and czars and it opened to the public in 1852. We were supposed to be admitted before the museum was open to the general public, but even so, we had to wait outside for a bit amid the street vendors. The most interesting thing for sale was a T-shirt with a McDonald's logo and a silhouette of Lenin superimposed over it. Everything could be purchased with the American dollar.

I will describe the Hermitage with one word: extraordinary. It is truly one of the great museums of the world.

We spent about three and one-half hours in the museum. We saw incredible art, architecture and sculpture. It surpassed Versailles outside of Paris. On the main floor, there were the rococo staircases, galleries, the throne room, and malachite room.

Then there were the paintings. Wow—such incredible talent. In the rooms where the impressionist paintings were hung, the windows were open. I'm not so sure this was a good idea.

Prior to leaving we had a few minutes in the museum's small gift shop where, oddly, everything thing had two prices, one in rubles, the other in dollars. We were particularly impressed with the quality of the goods. Mrs. C. wanted to buy a museum book and had to use a credit card, as we didn't have any dollars or rubles. On board we had been told that they would only take rubles and like I said, the ship's purser was not allowed to sell rubles. Bureaucracy.

Now it was time for lunch—at the *St. Petersburg Astoria Hotel*. We dined on vodka, caviar, champagne, salmon, and a salad. The hotel was furnished as if for royalty. Not "if": It was furnished for royalty and the extremely wealthy.

Near the hotel is St. Isaac's Cathedral—actually, church is probably a better word. We were able to walk to it. While it is not the size of some of the churches we have visited in other parts of Europe, it is a formidable building on both the outside and the inside. There are no pews in Russian churches; those who attend services stand—

sometimes for a couple of hours. The most impressive part of the church is a stained glass depiction of Jesus in flowing red robes. It is a restoration since the original was damaged in WWII. Even so, the church is said to have sustained only minor damage during the German siege of St. Petersburg during WWII. I'm not sure how that is possible.

I found it interesting that our guide used the word "Nazis" when referring to the Germans of WWII, not "Germans." The siege of St. Petersburg, then Leningrad lasted nearly two-and-a-half years until January 27th, 1944. It is a wonder that anything survived.

The traffic in St. Petersburg is formidable. Not because of the number of cars, compared to what we see at home in the US or in Europe . There aren't as many cars; it is just less organized. By this I mean that traffic signals are few and far between, so getting through intersections can be difficult at best. At most intersections where there are no traffic lights there are generally no signs indicating who has the right of way. In Rome there are lanes marked on the roads, and while they are often ignored, they do give traffic some semblance of order. Here in central St. Petersburg, there are often no lanes at all. It seemed like chaos. Not good.

Nesting Dolls

At a small market we stopped at along a canal, we found some interesting tourist curios, mostly nesting dolls. One of the more interesting dolls, obviously designed for American tourists, was Bill Clinton. Inside of

Bill, was Monica Lewinski, inside of Monica was Paula Jones, inside of Paula was Hillary. I found this terribly funny. There were Putin nesting dolls as well, but they made no sense to us at all.

St. Petersburg is a city of rivers, as it is situated on the delta of the River Neva. It is also very flat. I mention this because the rivers add to the expanse and flatness of the city. The rivers are a major form of transportation and as you can imagine, opening them only adds to the traffic problems. To solve this problem, the bridges open only when absolutely necessary and nightly between two and five in the morning—allowing goods and services to freely move about the city by water. If you are on one of the islands when the bridges are up, getting home or to your destination could prove to be a problem.

Spilled Blood

Across the street from the market we were taken to is the Church of Spilled Blood. Its name does not connote what you would think; it does not refer to the blood of Christ. Actually, the blood spilled was that of Tsar Alexander II, who was assassinated here in 1881. The church was begun in 1883 and it took nearly 25 years to complete. (As usual, there were funding problems.) The church's architecture is exactly what you would expect of a Russian church, with colored cupolas that are the swirling domes of the Muscovy design. We did not go in, there was an entrance fee, in rubles, and we had no rubles or dollars either. Rats.

Tiny Feet

For our second day in St. Petersburg our excursion was to Peterhof Palace, the sumptuous summer palace and grounds of Tsar Peter the Great.

The palace is truly opulent. We were able to visit both the palace and the grounds. It was stunning.

We had lunch in the *Orangrie*, a small restaurant on the Peterhof grounds. Here we were treated to salmon, cabbage soup, some dessert and, of course, vodka.

We had a tour of the grounds where our guide gave us interesting tidbits of information about Peter. For example, Peter was over six ft. tall and had disproportionately small feet, so he stuffed paper in his shoes to make his proportions better. He prided himself on being a master of many things, including surgery. We can't say how successful he was at this. But, if the tsar wanted to perform surgery on someone, who was going to stop him?

Peter also had a small building on the edge of Neva Bay that was perfect for a private *tête-à-tête*. The dictionary describes a tête-à-tête as a private conversation, but I am attributing more to it than that. It had a dining table, or portions thereof, that could be lowered into the basement where the food could be placed on it for dining and then raised back up to the diners. This was in case the diners did not want to see the servants, or the diners did not want to be seen *by* the servants. Let your imagination run wild.

Peter also had a small, more realistic and livable cottage a couple of miles down the road. He used this more often than the palace, or so we were told. We visited here as well and indeed found it more comfortable. And it also had a better view of the Baltic.

Generally speaking, I can't say that St. Petersburg is a pretty city; there is a lot of dull. The word that springs to mind is apathy; it is like the years of communist rule were a time when beauty and comfort held no value, the result being that it created a society that just doesn't care—about much of anything.

8. Greece

Greece feels old. Civilization may not have begun here, but in many ways it feels like it did. As such, somehow, it is seemingly appropriate that Athens is a dirty city. I don't mean that in a bad way. It's just that there is a lot of dirt. It falls out of the sky. It comes across from Africa and the Sahara and falls out of the sky.

Having been to Greece a few times and despite recent events that have made it more of a challenge, I still like the country and its people. As you know, the history is fascinating.

<u>You Cannot Die Here</u>

We were on a cruise through the Greek Islands where one of our stops was the small island of Delos in the Cyclades. The Cyclades is a group of islands in the Aegean Sea that form a rough circle to the south of Athens. Legend says that the Cyclades were sea nymphs that pissed off Poseidon, and he turned them into islands. Perhaps that is why they are generally such beautiful islands.

We arrived at Delos, the center of the Cyclades, around eight o'clock in the morning, to weather that was clear and slightly cool. Nice.

Delos is a sacred island. It is said to be the birthplace of Apollo and his sister Diana, also known as Artemis. It was also the site of an ancient trading city ideally situated, as I said, at the center of the Cycladic island group. During the Peloponnesian War and ostensibly at the suggestion of the Oracle of Delphi, the island was marked as sacred and it was decreed that no one should be allowed to die here. Not only that, but women were not allowed to give birth here. I presume pregnant women were not allowed on the island—don't want any accidental births creating new gods.

I find this no deaths and no births somewhat ironic considering there are numerous columns with the ruins of huge phalluses on them. Male genitalia seem to have been held in high regard. It would seem that you could have sex here, but not produce the results. Interesting indeed.

When we were there, wild flowers were in bloom. Everywhere there was purple statice (flowers) and orange poppies. The color against the almost white ruins of ancient villas and the vibrant blue sky was quite striking.

On Delos, it seems as though almost everything is *sacred*. There is the Sacred Lake, Sacred Precinct and the Theatre Quarter, where most of the ruins are found. There is the Terrace of Lions, the House of Dionysus, an archaeological museum and the Temple of Isis. And then there is the sacred phallus. I should note that the phalluses are not complete; it is only the lower part. The heads have been lopped off.

On the island, many of the houses, sanctuaries, and shops are well preserved, particularly considering they are 2,000 years old or more. In one of the recently excavated homes, we found a mosaic floor that was exquisitely intact. Today, no one lives on the island and not many ships visit, so unlike most of the other islands like Santorini and Mykonos, Delos was not crowded at all.

Santorini

We were on a cruise ship when we first visited the island on Santorini in the Aegean. Today, as you approach it, you see what is left, a small cluster of islands. It is but a shadow of its former self. The main island is shaped like a horseshoe, with the open end facing west, encircling a caldera. Across the caldera is a much smaller island named Therasia. In the center of the caldera are two tiny islands called Nea Kameni and Palea Kameni. They are hardly more than cinder cones that have arisen from the depths over the centuries since the eruption that took place around 1500 BC. Santorini still has minor shakes quite frequently, but fortunately, no mega eruptions seem imminent. The island is indeed the type of destination many people dream about—whitewashed houses lining the cliff face, gorgeous sunny days, beautiful sunsets, nothing moving in a rush, and good food.

The island is about 40 minutes by air south of Athens. Sailing into the caldera in the early afternoon we anchored at the base of rust-colored cliffs hundreds of feet high, just below the town of Fira, or *Thira* depending on the map or book you are looking at. Unlike most of our traveling companions, we were not eager to get up the cliff and see the town. We had no intention of heading off to any of the island's tourist spots because we had plans to spend more than just a few hours on the island. After our cruise we were coming back for a week.

Our goal was to experience Santorini, to do more than ride up the cliffs on a donkey, visit an archeological site, have lunch in the town, and buy some souvenirs as the day trippers do. We wanted to live there, to take our time exploring the island, to drink Greek wine, to watch the sun turn the sky blood red as it sets over the caldera, and to meet some of the people.

There are three ways of getting up the cliff and the town of Fira: by foot, by donkey, or by the funicular. Walking, I suspect, would take the better part of an hour (most likely more), and most people would be exhausted by the time they got to the top. And you would have to watch out for something donkeys have a tendency to leave behind. Taking the donkey is also slow, but generally less effort—for the rider, not the donkey. The last way is the funicular or cable car; it is by far the easiest. Once at the top in Fira, you stand on the edge of the cliffs and take in a vista that is a true vision of the quintessential Greek island.

After most of our fellow passengers had disembarked, we took the funicular up the cliff face to see if we could find our hotel for when we returned to the island—a place called Sun Rocks. We found the entrance to it. From the path at the top of the cliff, it was some 200-plus steps down to the hotel. We decided to wait until we returned to see it.

Arresting Cables

When we came back to Santorini on a short flight from Athens, I was a bit surprised that there are arresting cables stretched across the end of the runway—like on an aircraft carrier. Hmm.

As I said, we were staying at *Sun Rocks Villas-Apartments*, perched precariously on the cliffs of Firostefani, overlooking the caldera. From the hotel reception area to our room it was many, many, many steps. Our room was large, white, vaulted, cave-like, stark, and better than the brochure. It seemed to have an odor of fresh cement, so we left the doors open. The hotel is gorgeous, perched on the cliffs above the caldera.

In the late afternoon we walked into Fira on the path that is a promenade of sorts that runs along the top of the cliff. From the promenade you can look down on the hotels/villas as they cascade down the cliff face below. In town, we window-shopped and found a jewelry store that had interesting loose stones, fossils, geodes and such. They tried to sell us a lapis necklace for a mere $1,900— we passed. Here, unlike in the US, most gold is 20 or 24 karat. Gold of this higher karat is much softer than the eighteen karats we see in the US and is more susceptible to dents.

Like Key West, sunset is *the* thing in Santorini. Watching the orange sun set into the Mediterranean is what most people do at dusk, and we joined them. For us, this was all from the comfort of the terrace outside our room.

No Cars, No Dogs, Only Birds

We awoke to the sound of birds, not cars nor barking dogs, nor an alarm clock urging us to get ready to go ashore. This was our week to relax, to sleep late, and to just let the world go by. It is easy to let the world go by here; there is no television or radio. It is just the way we like it.

We had breakfast by the pool. The young lady there made us an omelet with ham and cheese, which is different from a ham and cheese omelet. The latter has the ham and cheese on the inside. She was so pleased with it and with herself, we didn't have the heart to tell her it was not exactly what we were expecting. The coffee however, was quite good. In fact, all the coffee I had in Greece was good. Avoid the orange juice. I'm not sure what it is— could be *Tang*. They do not have or import oranges here.

It took us a long time to get through breakfast.

It was late in the morning before we headed out to explore. Our exploration took us up (and I do mean up the cliffside) along the promenade to Imerovigli, the next little town, and way beyond that. Below Imerovigli, there is a peninsula of sorts with a large rock tower or crag on it called Skaros. We were somewhat surprised to see a path out to it, a path with people on it. It was midday and it was hot, as in very—"only mad dogs and Englishmen. . ." On the caldera side of Skaros is a small church, the one found on some of the most popular postcards in Santorini. Instead of attempting the arduous climb down to Skaros, we had lunch overlooking it.

Late in the afternoon, I walked up to the nearby mini-market and bought a bottle of Santorini wine—just a little something to sip on as we watched the evening's sunset. When I got to the promenade and glanced down at our pool, I noticed several women without their tops. No big deal—some Americans might be offended, but this is Greece, so it is completely acceptable.

That evening, as the sun went down, turning red in the western sky, we sat on our deck in the cool evening, enjoying our wine, and thinking it doesn't get much better than this.

Not an American

On the main road above the cliffs there was a rental car agency that our hotel host had told us about. Even though insurance was included with my credit card, it was part of the standard rental price, and I thought this a good idea.

With our car, we drove to Oia (pronounced *ee-a*) on the north end of the island and were fortunate enough to find a parking lot (what a concept, the antithesis of Athens). Oia is gorgeous! Mrs. C. was quite pleased with her shopping experience.

I will probably offend people with this but. . . While we were walking Oia's promenade, we managed to get behind Mr. Epitome of No Class. I thought to myself, "Please God, don't let him be American." He was big and fat, with his shirt unbuttoned and his big belly sticking out, a huge ugly unkempt handlebar mustache, ugly shorts (which did match his shirt), flip-flop shoes, and balding on the top with long hair in the back. To my relief he was not speaking English and was not American.

Lunch in Oia was excellent. We got some gyros at a little walk-up near the entrance to town and they were terrific. I am noting this because in Athens I was never able to find gyros. They were some of the best we've ever had. Could be because of where we were. We stopped at a different place for some dessert, a pastry, and a couple of drinks that ended up costing more than the gyros. They cost more because we sat down; sitting down makes food more expensive. In any case, it was good to sit in the shade and enjoy the view.

On the road back to Firostefani, we passed a large rock that was bigger than our car that had fallen from the cliff above onto the road. I didn't remember it being there on the way to Oia. Hmmm.

No sooner had we walked back into our room when it began to shake—an earthquake. I was not surprised. I was not alarmed. Santorini is, after all, a volcanic island. Mrs. C. said that she had felt one earlier that was similar in strength, but I was probably in the pool and didn't feel it. They both probably were less than 4-something on the Richter scale. I actually would have been surprised if we didn't have some sort of shake while we were there.

Once, during the night when I got up and went outside, I saw the moon, blood red, full and low in the western sky. It was unlike anything I had seen before, but I could not help but think how appropriate it would be in a Dracula movie.

Chock the Wheels

The next morning the weather was a bit cool and as we ate, we watched clouds moving up the side of the cliffs from the caldera. All the surrounding islands were obscured by clouds as well. In fact, Imerovigli, the next town, was not visible at all.

After breakfast, we headed south in the car. I'll note here that the car was far from the best rental car we've ever had. (But it was significantly better than the one on Moorea in Tahiti.) Just to be safe, I had chocked a wheel with a large rock in the parking lot where we had parked it during the night.

Our first sightseeing stop was the Boutari Winery. We actually bought something here, wine, an award-winning wine, although I'm not sure who issued the award. Anyway, the award-winning wine was not for export, but I was sure we could enjoy it with our evening sunset-watching.

A digression. While we were there, we ran into a couple that had been on our ship. (Santorini is a small island.) Somehow in talking to them we found out that they liked to go salmon fishing in Iceland. According to them, the best time to go to Iceland is in July or August when it can get up to 70, degrees, but usually it's in the 40s at this time of year. And, at that time of year the fields are usually covered with flowers.

Leaving the winery, we set off to find Akrotiri and Red Beach on the south side of the island. Akrotiri is an excavated Minoan archaeological site (town) from the Bronze Age. (To be discussed in a bit more depth shortly.) We knew we couldn't get in to Akrotiri because it is closed on Mondays, but it was on the way to the Red Beach, which was where we really wanted to go. We found Akrotiri and the beach was just beyond it. It was indeed a red beach, closer actually to a sort of rusty red. And it was the same as the high cliff face behind the beach. It wasn't, unfortunately, as neat as I expected.

Echoes off the Walls

After we left Red Beach, we headed towards Perissa on the southeast coast of the island. Along the way, just outside the turn off for the main road to Akrotiri, we stopped at a shop that sold extremely nice replicas of ancient Greek vases, plates, bowls and amphorae. Unlike the real ones, these weren't broken. It was a very nice shop.

Back in the car, we headed toward the town of Perissa when all of a sudden the car got very loud, it was almost like an explosion! The muffler on the car had blown out. I think you could hear us all over the southern part of the island.

We made enough noise to frighten cows, pigs, cats, children and the elderly. Those we didn't frighten, we annoyed.

We drove through Perissa with the sound echoing off the walls of the buildings we passed between. At the beach it was easy to find a place to park. You may have seen travel writer Rick Steves on a beach on Santorini—actually he's been to several of them, I think this is one of his favorites. We took a stroll along the shore water with the lapping waves at our feet, hoping the beach would get would get nicer as we went along. It didn't. It did seem to get hotter and there wasn't much of a breeze. There wasn't much to see and there were not very many people out and about—either on the beach or in any of the little restaurants and cafes. Tourist season doesn't start until the first of June. This was *the* black sand beach of the island; to me it was more like gray sand. And the area in general is geared more for those who are into camping.

We tried to sneak out of Perissa, driving slowly, hoping to make as little noise as possible. It didn't work. We could not be discreet in any way, shape, or form. Our goal was to get back to Thira before siesta time at two o'clock, when the car rental agency closed until five o'clock.

We made it. We switched cars and then walked into town in search of another excellent gyro for lunch. It was not to be found. Then it was time to head back to the hotel for the pool and our siesta. Our walk back was very slow; it was very hot.

That evening, while we had a car, we thought we'd drive to the town of Kamari, on the opposite side of the island, for dinner. We found our way to Kamari and parked the car, but we didn't know where to find the restaurant we were looking for. It was called *Camille Stephani*. We asked and were told that the restaurant was quite a ways down the beach. We decided to walk; it was a nice evening and all the places along the beachfront were lit up, like a boardwalk. It was fun. Dinner at the restaurant was quite good, but I found it odd that we heard very little English, at least along the beach. The most common language seemed to be German.

Beige on Khaki

The day after our muffler issue and while we still had a car, we headed for Akrotiri.

As I mentioned earlier, Akrotiri is the island's world renowned excavation site dating back to the third millennium BC, one in which you can feel the history, where you can peer into the past as if it were yesterday. The site is fairly large and it is covered, ostensibly to protect it from the elements. I think the cover is more to protect visitors from the often intense Santorini sun.

The entire site is monochromatic. Everything is one color: beige—ok, two colors, beige and khaki. If I'd had on khaki pants, I might had disappeared. It would appear anything and everything of interest, and worth seeing, had been removed to the museum in Athens. We were in and out in 15 minutes. It was a major disappointment.

We decided to head for *Ancient Thira*, the island's capital in classical times. It was near the town of Kamari, where we'd had dinner.

Because Santorini is a somewhat arid island, most places have water delivered by a truck at least twice a week. The water that comes from the faucet in the hotels is not drinkable, but it's fine for showers and such. The water you drink is bottled water. The water trucks look a lot like old gasoline trucks. Should we be concerned?

Ancient Thira

We found our way to Kamari over vineyard-covered hills and ostensibly through the villages of Exo Gonia and Mesa Gonia. If they were there, we never saw them; they must have been really small. We drove down into Kamari looking for a sign I had seen for Ancient Thira the night before. When we found the sign, we turned and faced the 1,100-foot high (369 meters) limestone rock of *Mesa Vouno*.

Atop *Mesa Vouno* is Ancient Thira. Fortunately, there is a road that takes you most of the way to the top. The road itself is steep, with 25 switchbacks, and is cobbled much of the way. You don't go very fast. In fact, you're lucky to get out of second gear. When you do get to the end of the road, there is a truly tiny parking lot, presumably for very small cars (like ours). The view is incredible; to the south is Perissa Beach and to the north the Kamari and Monolithos beaches. And the airport is to the east.

At the edge of the parking area, a trail leads further up *Mesa Vouno* towards the actual Ancient Thira site. The first stop is at a small plateau where there is a sanctuary. We didn't know if this was Ancient Thira or not. We did see that there were a few people on a trail that led up further still, so we followed. We were glad we did. We found Ancient Thira. Perched atop the mountain were the remains of a small city, Thira. It was occupied in the 6th and 7th centuries BC. To us, it was quite similar to Delos, an island mentioned earlier off the coast of Mykonos only without the phallic sculpture. Wow. Ancient Thira has it all over Akrotiri. What a view.

I am noting here that the hike up to Thira from the parking lot is substantial. Although, Mrs. C. still had metal in her ankle from a break six months earlier and she did fine.

During the drive back to Thira we encountered mule traffic. Mules apparently have the right-of-way. If they want to cross the road, you go around them. They do not move for you or see you coming. This is also true if you're on foot. You get out of their way.

Speaking of mules. . . When you come into Santorini by cruise ship, you will likely be tendered ashore just below the town of Thira that sits high on a cliff above the caldera. Ferry passengers come into the Santorini Ferry Port of Athinios south of town. Once on shore, you have two options for getting into town, the funicular or mule. I suppose you could walk up the mule path, but this is not recommended. The mules leave deposits along the way. At the end of the day, the mules are let loose to return to their stable, where their food is, by themselves. They know where the stable is, and you don't want to get in their way.

Santorini Notes

At the end of the day, it is quite pleasant to just sit and enjoy a glass of wine and watch the sun go down over the caldera. It can get cool rather quickly, so a sweater might be a good idea as the temperature can drop rather rapidly.

This might be out-of-date information, but we found that the toilets on the island do not accept toilet paper. Used toilet paper goes in the little covered wastebasket next to the commode. It is taken away every day and doesn't smell.

What is the difference, you may reasonably ask, between Thira and Fira, are they the same? Well, sort of. Fira *generally* refers to the main town overlooking the caldera while Thira is the name of the whole island of Santorini. The main town is often referred to Thira. Well that cleared that up. Not.

Inappropriate Shoes

A hard rain woke us around 6 a.m., which I felt was a little odd for Santorini—a fairly arid island. Due to the weather, we had second thoughts about going on a boat excursion that would take us around the caldera, but decided to go anyway.

We planned to catch the boat for our caldera tour in Fira but found a couple pastry shops that needed our attention; we gave it to them by acquiring a small assortment of Greek pastries and a coffee. Once we ate, we took the cable car down to the old port at the bottom of the cliffs, where we were to meet our boat. It is referred to as the old port because there is a new port a few miles south called *Athinios*. Athinios is where most of the local fishing boats, along with all sorts of other boats, tie up. Everyone says it is an unattractive little town, so it is perhaps best that we didn't have to go there.

We found our boat, and it was not exactly what we expected. We thought we would be going on a sailboat like we had seen in the caldera doing the sunset cruise. This was not to be. Our boat was a double-decked motor vessel that held a good number of people. We boarded, sat in the back, and set off at 10:30.

Our first stop was the volcanic island of Nea Kameni in the center of the caldera. It is basically a cinder cone of black volcanic rock—primarily obsidian. Plant life on the island is practically nonexistent. We were in luck because by the time we got there, the clouds had burned off and it was getting hot. The majority of the intrepid people on the boat went traipsing up the trail to the top on Nea Kameni, a steep climb of over a mile. We went only as far as the first plateau, about half way up. There were benches here and from where we sat, we could look back on Santorini and watch the others on their arduous climb. Among the travelers headed up the trail was a trio of Japanese girls who were dressed extraordinarily nice for climbing steep, rocky trails. In addition to the nice clothes, they all looked to have on expensive, high-heeled, *extremely inappropriate shoes.* I notice things like this now, especially after my Shirley's broken ankle the previous year.

At the next little island, Palea Kameni, there were hot springs bubbling up in a little bay—a very little bay. The boat anchored, and those who were so inclined dove off the boat. Those who went in the water did not make yummy noises like, "Ohhh, this is wonderful." So I didn't go in. While they were swimming, I fell asleep on the boat railing.

Next, we went to the island of Thirasia, across the caldera from Santorini. Here, we docked at the base of a cliff wall, just like on our island. There also were mules here to take travelers to the town of Manolas above, or you could stay along the water and have lunch at *Captain John's* like we did. Captain John's had good *tzatziki sauce*—good on everything. Back on the boat, we left mid-afternoon and headed towards Oia. I'm not sure if the well-dressed young ladies went up to Manolas, but we did not see them at Captain John's. I can't picture them riding the mules.

We had a stop at Oia on the north end of the main island to let a few people off and then headed back for the old port. It was nice to be out on the water where we could look up at the cliffs and the see the tiny buildings that lined the rim of the caldera, one of which was our hotel.

When we arrived back in the old port, there were four cruise shops at anchor, so we knew Fira would be crowded. Before our assent, Shirley had to check out the few shops that were there in the old port. While she shopped, I admired, no drooled, over a number of beautiful sailboats moored (stern in) at the quay. It must be nice.

That evening we watched our last Santorini sunset and then set out to find some dinner. We ate at the *Sphinx* restaurant in Fira. Dinner was very good, one of our best.

A digression on inappropriate shoes. . . Italy has recently banned flip-flops and sandals on the paths between the villages of Cinque Terre; they can be quite rugged. It seems that far too frequently tourists wearing inappropriate shoes are finding themselves in need of rescue. Here, the wrong kind of shoes can result in hefty fines.

On a different trip in Greece, we had traveled from Ephesus in Turkey to the Greek island of Patmos across a narrow strait in the eastern Mediterranean. Ephesus was a Roman city mentioned in the Bible's Book of Revelation written by Saint John the Apostle. John lived in Ephesus for a time. The connection here is that John wrote the *Book of Revelation* in a cave on the island of Patmos.

Today Patmos is often a destination for Christian pilgrimages. We were not part of a pilgrimage; we were part of a small group that had a walking tour of various locations of interest on the island, including the Cave of the Apocalypse. Our guide was a lovely young lady, fashionably dressed, with high-heeled shoes—for walking on cobblestones. Again, totally inappropriate shoes.

<u>Mykonos</u>

Mykonos is some six miles from Delos and is more popular, it is quite *the* tourist spot. We had to anchor quite some distance from the harbor due to high winds. From our anchoring, you could see the town across a white-capped bay.

Mykonos is very much what you'd imagine and what you'd want a Greek island to be. There are whitewashed buildings with brightly painted doors, and hanging bougainvillea and geraniums lining the small streets, most of which are too small for cars. And, it is windy; the wind between the buildings seemed to be 30 to 40 mph or more. The buildings seemed to act as a funnel or venturi, increasing the velocity of the winds significantly.

During the course of our wanderings, we bought a couple of Greek cotton sweaters and stopped in at a little bar called *Mykonos Aroma* for a coffee and pastry. (It could be that we just wanted to get out of the wind.)

While Mrs. C. was window-shopping, I set off to find Pete the (pink) pelican, mascot of Mykonos. He was down by the bay—completely unfazed by the wind. Interestingly, the wind was not as strong at the water's edge. This was a number of years ago so Pete may not be there anymore, or, there is a new Pete.

On the way back to the ship, Mrs. C. shopped. Unlike in Italy where I had had too much wine when she went shopping after dinner, here I was happy to help her. This means that I offered up my opinion. She bought an inexpensive necklace and earrings. Whether or not my opinion was taken into consideration remains to be seen. At dinner the next evening, we found out just how cheap they really were; the gold had already started to wear off the earrings.

We loved Mykonos; we'd come back in a heartbeat.

When we got back aboard ship, we noted that as the cruise wore on, we were seeing more and more injured people.

9. Ireland

We found Ireland to be a wonderful place, but they drive on the left, so you need to be careful just crossing the road. This chapter, though short, describes just a little bit about our experiences in Ireland.

People talk a great deal about the food in Italy and France, but rarely about Ireland. When we traveled in Ireland, we found the food to be quite good. In fact, each night we found that dinner was at least as good as, if not better than, the night before.

You Need To Come Get Me

In the early 1800s I suspect that monks, and people in general, did not bathe very often. I also suspect that they were not big on doing laundry, either. I bring this up because monks, who created Jameson Whiskey, originally made it as a perfume. I wonder why? Then they found it was better to drink.

While in Dublin, I thought it would be good to learn about in Irish whiskey. So while Mrs. C. napped, I went down to the bar for a lesson.

The barman was the bar supervisor and seemed quite pleased when I told him of my quest. He placed a flight of three whiskeys in front of me and told me how they were made and the differences between them. Jameson was the strongest, a second was milder but with more of an aftertaste, and a third was milder still but with more of a nose. I preferred the Jameson, as it is closer to the Canadian blended whisky that I prefer here in the US. After my sampling, I had a Jameson and 7-Up.

I did not go back to the room, instead I ordered some bar food to go with my drink and moved to a table in the nearby bar. Fortunately there was a telephone at the end of the bar. I called Mrs. C. in the room and told her she had better come down to the bar and get me, as my whiskey lesson had been a bit too successful.

Driving in Ireland

We started our Ireland visit in Dublin, where after a couple of days we rented a car for the rest of our tour. From Dublin, we headed south to Kilkenny, with a stop at Powerscourt, located in County Wicklow, it is a large country estate known for its house and landscaped gardens. It is worth a visit. Next it was on Waterford, home of the Waterford Crystal factory. From there we drove on to Cork, which I found to be an extraordinarily confusing place to drive, before heading to Kenmare, which isn't. From Kenmare, we headed north through the Killarney National Park to Dingle on the Dingle Peninsula. We did not drive the Ring of Kerry because we had read that the Dingle Peninsula was better.

Driving in Ireland can be a challenge, not because they drive on the left, but because a great many of the roads are so incredibly narrow, at least to us Americans.

Another complication is that the roads frequently have high hedges next to them so there is no shoulder that you can pull off on to. From my perspective, if there was a line in the center of the road, it was a major highway. Even so, it is a fabulous country.

We like staying in bed & breakfasts, and the ones we stayed at in Ireland were exceptional. Sometimes a bed & breakfast can be a bit more than a hotel, like the one we stayed at in the town of Adare, county Limerick, the *Adare Manor*. This is a Manor House, which is not quite a castle. The manor house was built in the 1830s and was once owned by the Earl of Dunraven. It is made of stone and sits along the River Maigue amid 840 acres. It has a few eccentricities, including a turreted entrance tower at one corner of the building rather than in the center. It has 52 chimneys (one to commemorate each week of the year), 75 fireplaces and 365 leaded-glass windows (one for each day of the year).

I want to make a special note about the Foynes Flying Boat Museum on the River Shannon not too far from Adare. The museum is dedicated to the Flying Boats that Pan Am used to fly around the world back in the 1930s and '40s, when air travel was in its infancy and was something really special. The museum is small but good with a great deal of history for aviation buffs.

Our last residence in Ireland was just outside the town of Shannon, in a village called New Market on Fergus. The Fergus is a river that passes Bunratty Castle a little farther inland. Finding B&Bs can be a bit more challenging than finding a hotel in a city, but in this case, there were signs, in English, and we were able to find our B&B, the Carrygerry House, quite easily. The house is a bit out in the country, within sight of the Shannon Airport and the Fergus estuary.

Green and White

Our stay at the Carrygerry House was quite nice, and it was very well situated, even it if is a little off the main roads. I must say that the dinners we had there were excellent. We thought ourselves lucky to be able to do this, as most B&B's don't serve dinner.

As I said, the B&B is near, relatively speaking, the Shannon Airport.

One night as I got up to go to the bathroom, I noticed that my wife looked a bit pale as she slept, not healthy. Then as I came out of the bathroom, she looked slightly green. Then she turned the pale again. Was she turning into a ghost? I turned to look out the window and saw, in the distance, a couple of miles away, a beacon on top of the tower at the Shannon airport. Aviation beacons alternate between white and green.

Cows

Not too far from our B&B is a hotel called Dromoland. It is a castle, and is very popular with the golfing set. The month of May, when we were in Ireland, is a very big golfing month, and reservations at Dromoland were hard to come by. Nonetheless, we were able to secure dinner reservations in their top-notch restaurant. We had to check it out.

As we headed out to dinner, we encountered a road obstacle a short distance from our B&B. Cows. In Ireland the roads are, as I said, quite narrow, and we could not get past a small heard of cows ambling down the road. A young boy was, in theory, guiding the lead cow down the road by its tail. It was not working well. We moved to the left to pass the cow, but the cow did not want to let us pass, it moved to the left too. The boy would attempt to steer it right, but the cow would only look over its shoulder, see us, and move to get in our way. We would drop back. We tried the cow's right. No luck. On the third try, I got the car just abreast of the cow before it looked left. Bonk. It bumped its nose right into our side mirror. Talk about a surprised cow. She was not a happy cow and maybe had a sore nose. Shirley mouthed "Sorry." out the window as we squeezed on by. The young boy just waved us on.

At Dromoland, we were shown into dinner in the grand drawing room. On the walls were pictures of the past residents of the castle, the Earls and Barons of Thomond. In fact, according to the *maître d'*, it was the 15th Baron who watched over the diners in the dining room. Part of the fun of the dining experience here was watching the people. There was the athlete with his trophy girlfriend, the golfers, some who'd had good days and those who had not. Then there was the couple that spoke only to the waiter and never said a word to each other.

While dinner was wow, I thought our B&B had the edge.

Manhattan

In Dingle, we stayed at a very nice place called The Castlewood House, with hosts Nancy and Brian. As it turns out, Brian used to be the manager of the hotel where we stayed in Dublin. We had a room looking out over Dingle Bay which I found to be oddly soothing.

In the early evening we walked into town to find some dinner. We ended up at the *Smokehouse* restaurant where we had Steak & Guinness pie as opposed to Steak and Ale pie. This one was better because it wasn't just ale, it was Guinness.

After dinner, we set out to find some traditional Irish music, some *trad*. We found some, at a pub recommended by Nancy our host. It was here that we met Melissa and Martin from Boston. We also met Jack the jockey, a local fellow from nearby Limerick. Jack was there with his mates celebrating the Limerick (Munster) Rugby team win at its most recent match. At least this is what Melissa and Martin told us. I could not understand Jack, even though he was, in theory, speaking English. Jack was at least three sheets to the wind, perhaps four or five.

In the pub, the way it works is that you go to the bar to get your drink and bring it back to the table. And when you order a Guinness (what else would you order?), the barman draws it and then sets it on the bar. You do not pick up the glass; you wait for the foam to go down a bit, between three and five minutes, and then the barman or barmaid finishes filling the glass. You must be patient to drink Guinness in Ireland. Mrs. C., not being a beer drinker, had a *Shandy* (beer and lemonade). She was not impressed.

Back at the table, the conversation with Jack the jockey was getting stranger. About all I could make out was the word Manhattan. I don't know if he knew someone from Manhattan, thought we were from Manhattan, or he was working on the Irish version of the Manhattan project. Thank God the music started.

The music was indeed Irish, but not exactly what we wanted. It was only a guitar and an accordion. We wanted a fiddle and an Irish drum. Even so, it was great fun.

When I went back to the bar for a refill, I met a couple from Seattle (like me). They did not give me their names; they must have been traveling incognito. I bought Shirley a Bulmer's hard cider; this is what Melissa was drinking. She liked it very much and will likely have it again.

When I returned to the table, Jack got a call from his mates asking where he was. They had moved on to another pub. This is what I presume was the gist of the conversation because Jack said he had to go find his mates, at least that is what Melissa and Martin told us he said.

We left the bar around 11 o'clock and walked back to our room. It was quite cool, and but was still a faint bit of light in the sky. We did not see Jack or any of his mates again.

A note about the roads on the Dingle Peninsula. Most of the signs are in Gaelic, which bears little resemblance to English. So when you see a sign that does have both, it is a good idea to make a mental note of your Gaelic destination—if this is even possible.

No Coaches

Heading north of New Market on Fergus, past Ennis, you enter an area known as The Burren.

"Burren" is a Gaelic word meaning rocky place. This is an apt description, and the farther north you go, the rockier it seems to become. North of the Burren is Galway Bay and to the west is the Atlantic Ocean. The Burren is quite a large area, about 250 square kilometers.

Geologically, the Burren are limestone hills dissected by joints or fissures running north and south. I know this because I had a compass in my pocket to check. Also the land was subjected to extreme glaciation a mere 10,000 years ago. It seems like only last week.

Shirley had read of a perfumery of the Burren, located near the town of Carran. She wanted to visit. Their claim to fame was that they made perfumes from the flowers and other resources of the local terrain. We apparently missed a turn somewhere and ended up in Kilfenora, where, at the tourist information office, we were able to obtain a more detailed map that set us straight. (A figure of speech because I do not think there are any really straight roads in the Burren.)

Backtracking a bit and then heading north again, we took the second road to Carran, thinking it would be shorter. It might have indeed been shorter, but it was steeper and significantly more harrowing because of the narrowness of the road.

Once we were in Carran (which is three buildings), we followed signs to the perfumery, and it was here that we noticed a sign at the turn off that read, "No Coaches." We were not a bus, so we'd be ok. Wrongo. Shortly after turning onto the road for the perfumery we came over a rise to find a coach, a bus, with his backup lights on. We could not believe our eyes—the road is hardly wide enough for a car, let alone a bus. I guess he had not seen the sign.

The driver got out and motioned us over to a spot where we could back off the road a bit. He then proceeded to back his bus on by us. I pulled my outside mirror in to give more room, but even so he had less than six inches clearance as be backed by. He was good, but he obviously should have heeded the sign.

Out of Guinness

While this anecdote took place in Scotland, it does, in a way, relate to Ireland, so I include it here.

While in Edinburgh, we stopped into a pub for lunch, the Jekyll & Hyde. When we ordered our food, I asked for a beer, a Guinness. They were out. My thought was, "How can any pub, even though it is in Scotland not Ireland, be out of Guinness?" This was, to me, inconceivable.

Okay, this was odd enough, but a few months later I was talking to someone at work and I detected what I thought was a slight Scottish accent. I asked if he was Scottish and he said that indeed he was. I related the story of how I had been in Edinburgh a few months earlier and how I had gone into a pub, and they were out of Guinness.

He said, "My family is part owner of a pub in Edinburgh. What was the name of the pub?

"The Jekyll & Hyde." I replied. It was his family's pub. What are the odds?

10. England

We have been to London several times, and it is one of our favorite cites. I think this is because it is so easy to get around. And, every time we go it seems like there are new things to see and do. What follows are a couple experiences and observations. To us Americans, the British seem a bit different.

The London Underground

My wife and I were in the Gloucester tube stop in the London underground, waiting for either a green or yellow line train to come along. We were discussing which would be best to get us to our destination. We had not made any decision when a train arrived. The doors opened, people got off and I got on.

Anyone who has ridden on a subway knows that the doors on the train are open for just seconds. I was onboard when the doors closed. Shirley was not. I saw her through the glass as I turned around and the train started to depart. She looked totally surprised that I was on the train and she wasn't. I mouthed the words, "I'll meet you at the next station." I did. I think this may happen more often than you would think, particularly with tourist.

Scottish Beef

We left our hotel at 6:30 p.m. and took the underground to Monument station. We were to have dinner at dusk at the Fenchurch restaurant in the Sky Garden atop an office building in London near the river.

Once off the train and above ground, we used our phone's GPS to find Fenchurch Street. When exiting the underground, I am often confused about which way to go. I don't think this is just me. Even with the GPS I felt lost.

When we found the right building and were told that the entrance to the restaurant was on the side. Obvious, right? We checked in on the ground floor and had to go through security before we were allowed to take the elevator to the 35th floor. It is called the Sky Garden because there is a garden on the top floors of the building. The 35th floor is a bar/lounge area with expansive views looking out over London. We checked in (again) and were told that our reservation was at the restaurant two floors up. We took the elevator up to the 37th floor and the Fenchurch restaurant where we were seated at the bar.

While the menu was not all that big, it did have a few good items. The only thing that Shirley found appealing was something called the Scottish Rib Chop for two. Our waiter told us that even though our entrée was a scotch rib chop, the beef did not come from Scotland. It came from a farm in southern England owned by the restaurant. Hmm. We were given some appetizers and a glass of wine to start the evening.

When dinner came, it was huge and included not only the rib chop but a rocket salad, asparagus, and fries. The rib chop was quite rare and came with two sauces, hollandaise and a bone marrow sauce. Everything was quite rich and extraordinarily delicious. I tried to find the less rare pieces of the chop for Mrs. C., but even with it being rare, she was quite pleased. We passed on dessert; we were too full. Dinner had been fabulous.

As we were getting our check the lights were coming up in the city below us. The views were quite good and we spent quite a bit of time taking pictures of the city. The Tower of London was almost just below us.

By the time we left it was about 9 o'clock and it still wasn't yet fully dark. We made our way back to the Monument underground station and headed back for our hotel. It had been a delicious dinner and a memorable evening even though the Scottish Beef was, in my opinion, not really Scottish.

Afternoon in the Park

We took a tour from London out to Oxford and Stratford upon Avon. (Having a car in London is not a good idea.) We had a guide/narrator on the ride out to Oxford who tried to explain the British school and university system that to us seemed supremely odd even with the explanation. Our first stop was Oxford were we were able to see what was the inspiration for many of the places in Harry Potter's Hogwarts School for Wizards. Next our tour took us into Stratford upon Avon (the Avon is a river) through acres of yellow canola fields and bright blue flowers found only in Britain. Along the way, our guide told us some of the details of Mr. Shakespeare's life.

William was born on April 23, 1564. His father was a leather merchant and his mother, Mary Arden, was a landed heiress. He married Anne Hathaway and when he died, he bequeathed his second best bed to her. His second best bed? Who got his best bed? Why did his wife not get the best bed? It makes you wonder.

After touring the Shakespeare birthplace cottage, we found some delicious pasties for lunch walked over to the nearby river to eat them. When we sat down it felt like we part of the post-impressionist Georges Seurat painting *A Sunday Afternoon on the Island of La Grande Jatte* (a.k.a. *Afternoon in the Park)*. It was surreal.

Leaving Stratford upon Avon, we headed to nearby Warwick Castle. Some segments of *Harry Potter* were filmed there. I suppose that there are a very large number of places where *Harry Potter* segments were filmed. Nonetheless, Warwick Castle is indeed a castle. A fortification has been on this spot since the 11th century. Some of the rooms were decorated as they might have been in medieval times. In the castle's main dining room, they were setting up for a big dinner that evening. Alas, our invitations had been lost in the mail.

Speaking of mail, the term "*post*" comes from posts that used to be in place on the edge of villages. There, mail bags would be hung and picked up by riders, hence the term "to post a letter."

We came across an archery and crossbow display. We learned that there was amour that could stop a bolt from a crossbow—but the victim would still likely die due to internal organ hemorrhaging as a result of the impact. (Isn't this useful information?)

11. Germany & Austria

The time we have spent in Germany and Austria has been mostly along their rivers. My two favorite cites in this area are Berlin and Vienna. It would be inappropriate to mention Berlin without saying something about the beer. I enjoyed the beer in Berlin, and in Germany in general quite a bit, much more so than the beer in Denmark.

Bones

It was raining in the morning we arrived in the town of Speyer on the Rhine. It is not a large town, but it has approximately 50,000 inhabitants. I find it interesting that throughout Europe, when describing the population of a place, they use the word "inhabitants." In the US, the word used is usually "people" or "population." *Inhabitants* make me wonder if the number given includes animals as well.

Speyer has a cathedral. One made primarily from brick and not stone. The cathedral has items of note, but not like the relics and fame of the Cologne upon Avon. Well, not exactly.

It seems that the Speyer Cathedral has relics that are a bit different, the bones of several emperors and kings. After accumulating the remains of several noteworthy individuals over the centuries, the cathedral management decided to hire the preeminent bone-cleaner for a big event that was coming up. Now, the cleaner was getting on in years, but management knew he would do a good job. He did. The unfortunate part was that he did not label whose bones were whose. So while they still have the same bones, they are now mixed up. Oops.

Excommunication

Then there was the story of a local king who did something that pissed off the Pope. The king was excommunicated. In the 17th century, being king and excommunicated was not a good thing. In penance, the king walked to Rome and pleaded with the Pope to un-excommunicate him. (I am sure some money changed hands as well.) In the end, the king was no longer excommunicated.

Did the king learn his lesson? Apparently not. Years later he pissed off the Pope again and was ex-communicated again. He was not up to doing penance now and, being excommunicated, he could not be buried in consecrated ground. Big problem. When he died they found a small part of the cathedral, a shed on the side that had not been consecrated, so they buried him there in the tool shed next to the cathedral. His son, being a good son, undertook the effort to get his father un-excommunicated again and back in the church's good graces so that he could be reburied in consecrated ground. He pulled it off, and the disobedient (for lack of a better word) king was finally dug up and reburied in consecrated ground.

On a cleanliness note, this cathedral was far and away much cleaner than the one in Cologne. Inside, as a very small group, we pretty much had the place to ourselves so we could explore as we wished. Very nice indeed.

Richard the Lionheart

We were visiting Dürnstein in Austria where our guide, a fellow named Aaron, told us about Richard the Lionheart. How would Richard the Lionheart come up in Austria, you ask? Well, he was imprisoned here in 1193 and 1194. Aaron told us that Richard (aka Richard I) was not a nice guy.

It seems that after his third crusade to the Holy Land, Richard was on his way back to England when he was captured by Duke Leopold of Austria. He had pretty much pissed off most of his fellow royals during the crusades, including Philip of France, and of course Leopold.

Richard had, according to our guide, thrown down Leopold's flag that he had placed on captured land in the Middle East, saying that Leopold was unworthy and other not nice things, most likely about his birth lineage.

It is almost Christmas in 1192, and Richard is trying to sneak back to England via central Europe. He needed to get back to England because Prince John, his brother, was usurping his power. This is the Prince John of Robin Hood fame. The weather is awful, and he is held up on the outskirts of Vienna near Dürnstein. He had come ashore near Venice and was taking the land route back to England. He was attempting to avoid France, presumably because the relationship he had once had with the King of France had soured.

Richard is traveling incognito, but being Mr. Aristocrat, he had a tendency to make aristocrat demands, like roast chicken or beef for his dinner. He sent his underlings to fetch his food, and they attempt to pay with unusually large gold coins. Some think that his minions still referred to him as "Sire," and this was overheard.

Cutting to the chase, Leopold hears about this and investigates. Much to his pleasure, he finds Richard and takes him hostage. In the end, Richard was ransomed for an enormous sum, 150,000 marks, that many say was well more that the GDP of England at that time. Richard's mother, Eleanor of Aquitaine, contributed much to the ransom by selling all of Richard's goods and taking monies from churches and monasteries. Prince John was not inclined to help. Richard was eventually released in February 1194, but how he got back to England while avoiding France, I do not know. Aaron told us that it is believed some of the ransom silver is still in Austrian coins of today.

12. Switzerland

Whenever I think of Switzerland, I cannot help but think of a book my grandmother gave me back in the early 1970s. The book is called *Return to the Alps* and is full of extraordinary photographs; I remember when she gave it to me, I thought wow, I want to go there. Now, decades later, I still say wow when I look at the book. It is this memory that gave me the impetus to visit Switzerland.

When I started looking into visiting Switzerland, it seemed obvious that the way to do this was by rail. As it turned out, this was indeed the thing to do.

Getting to Lucerne

On a Rhine river cruise, we arrived in Basel, Switzerland, early in the morning, before we awoke. Basel was our termination and disembarkation point. We had asked the concierge to arrange to have a taxi pick us up and take us to the train station.

When we got in the cab, the first thing our driver said was, "Where to?"

I said, "The train station."

He said, "Which one?"

Marvelous; how was I to know? I told him that we were headed to Lucerne, hoping that he'd know which one to take us to. He did. So off we went. (Note that we spoke English.)

It never occurred to me that there would be multiple train stations—even though most European cities have more than one. Our ticket read Basel SBB, so it confirmed that the station to which our driver was indeed taking us to the right one.

At the station, we checked the reader board but did not see a train to Lucerne that left at 9:00 o'clock, so we decided that the one that left at 9:15 must be our train. The board said that our train was to depart from platform 15. This is what we hoped the board said; it was not in English. Fortunately, numbers are the same in any language so how wrong could we be.

We were able to find our train, our car, and our assigned seats. Cool. Our big question was, do we need to get our tickets stamped by some machine before getting on board, even though we were already on board. The French are very, very fussy about this. I found someone to ask and was told that our type of tickets did not need to be stamped. Cool, again.

Our train left at precisely 9:15—the Swiss are very precise about this sort of thing. The trip took only a couple of hours including several two-minute stops in route.

Upon our arrival at the Lucerne station, the first thing on our agenda was to find our hotel. I went into the tourist office at the station and asked a young lady at the desk where I might find the *Hotel Waldstaetterhof Swiss*. She pointed over my shoulder said, "Right there." How convenient is that? Shirley had booked the hotel online and chose one close to the train station. I guess we did not realize how close.

Ghosts and Dragons

Lucerne sits on Lake Lucerne—imagine that—in central Switzerland. The setting is gorgeous where the town and the lake are surrounded by the Alps.

One of the touristy things to do in Lucerne is to go up to the top of Mt. Pilatus, located just above and to the west of town. The weather on the day we chose to go did not bode well, alternating rain and clouds; the chance that the summit would be socked in was thought to be high.

We checked with the folks at the hotel's front desk and they told us we should talk to the ticket office in front of the train station. They had better hopes for the weather, but not much. They told us that we could either take a train or boat to the base of the cog railway, which would then take us up to the top of the 7,000-foot peak, or we could take a bus to a gondola station and go up that way. The gondola was not currently in operation due to high winds so it was not a valid option.

We asked when the boat left and were told, "In 15 minutes."

The boat was a good choice. It takes about 90 minutes to get to the cog railway at Alpnachstad, but being out on the lake, the *Vierwaldstättersee* as the lake is known locally, was wow. Spectacular is an understatement. We were indeed in the Alps, just like in my book.

The round trip, on the boat or train, and the cog railway up to the top of Mt. Pilatus was 200 CHF (Swiss Francs). We went 1st class, which meant that we were able to sit on the upper deck of the lake steamer, with a table and food and drink if so desired. There were a few stops in route to Alpnachstad, but instead of seeing them as slowing down the excursion on the lake, they actually enhanced it.

Disembarking at Alpnachstad, we walked about 100 yards from the boat to the railway car that was to take us up the mountain. The trip up the side of the mountain is steep—45° at minimum, often more. This is why it is a cog train; it would be far too steep for a regular train. The ride up took about 40 minutes and we stopped only once, to let the cars headed down pass by.

As we approached the top, there was fresh snow. Good thing we had dressed warm.

At the top, the weather changed rapidly and constantly. The mountain, Pilatus, was named after a local legend that Pontius Pilate is buried there. Hmm. His ghost is said to sometimes make appearances. Perhaps on a day like this. Why on earth would he be buried here? According to some accounts, he was either ordered to be killed by Caligula or he went into exile. Exile here? This could account for the ghost said to dwell here.

Then there is the dragon. In late medieval times a dragon was said to live on the mountain. The benevolent dragon with healing powers was first seen in 1421 or 1499, depending on which legend you prefer. I was curious as to how the local people determined the dragon was benevolent. I never found out.

We saw neither ghost nor dragon. Disappointing.

What we did see was that within the peak, a tunnel has been chiseled out that provides overlooks and/or windows on to the valley below. The low ceiling of the tunnel was covered in icicles—that dripped. It was just above freezing and the floor of the tunnel was mostly ice, so it was very slick. There were a couple of the viewpoints that opened out to a view of the valley. These viewpoints are on a sheer side of the peak that plunges down a couple thousand feet. While there were guardrails, it was not for the faint of heart. If you slipped and went under the lower rail, you were toast. From the vista windows, I could see that the cable cars coming up from the valley below were running, so I presume the winds had died down a bit.

In the main building that is at the top of the cog railway, we found a small place to have lunch: bratwurst and fries. What else would we have?

We had the option of going back to town via the cable car, but opted for the boat. So we took the train back down.

Back at Alpnachstad, we had another choice. We could take the boat back to Lucerne or the train. The train would be faster, but we thought the boat would be more comfortable and provide better views and we could have a glass of wine on the way. It was once again simply awesome.

There's Not Much Air Here

Later that same trip, we were staying in Grindelwald in the Swiss Alps and when we awoke we were pleased to find that it was not raining as it had been the night before. It was cloudy, but there was blue in places. You can't see a lot of the sky here because the mountains take up so much of it. It reminded me of a former coworker who did not like to go to Florida. He said, "There's too much sky"

Because it was not raining, we thought this was to be our best opportunity to go to the Jungfrau, a mountain that is one of the highest points in Europe. After breakfast, we bought train tickets to the Jungfrau at our hotel. They were expensive, but after you see what you have to go through to get there, you understand why.

We walked down to the train station at the other end of the town. Here there is only one station but two railroad lines. One goes to Interlaken and the other to Kleine Scheidegg.

Kleine Scheidegg is a high mountain pass that sits below and to the west of the major mountains of the area, the *Eiger*, the *Mönch*, and the *Jungfrau*. These peaks are in the Bernese Oberland area of Switzerland. It is via Kleine Scheidegg that you get to the Jungfrau.

In Grindelwald we boarded the 9:17 train to Kleine Scheidegg. It was a cog railway train. Not all the trains in Switzerland use a cog track—only those that have a lot of climbing to do. And we did. The trip to Kleine Scheidegg took us about 40 minutes.

At Kleine Scheidegg, we changed trains for the final leg of our journey up to the top of the Jungfrau, through the mountain. Not long after leaving this transfer station, we went into a tunnel that took us to a station at the top of the mountain known as the *Jungfraujoch*. It is the highest railway station in Europe. We stopped twice along the way to peer out of windows cut in the mountainside, but it was too socked in to see anything. Well, I guess we did see something: clouds.

The Jungfrau, or "young maiden" in German, is, as I said, one of the highest peaks in the Alps at 13,642 feet, and it's billed as the "Top of Europe." The Jungfrau is right next to the Eiger, the "old man," at 13,025 feet and the Mönch, the "monk," at 13,474 feet.

The *Jungfraujoch* is a large building complex built into and on top of a rocky outcropping very near the summit of the Jungfrau. It has a couple of restaurants, a gift shop, an ice cave, and observation platforms. If you plan to go outside, as we did, it is best to dress warm. When we were there at the end of May, it was well below freezing. The temperature inside the complex was cool, but not too bad.

One thing we did notice and feel at the high altitude was the lack of oxygen. After walking from the train into the building, Shirley had to rest for a bit. I, on the other hand, started up the stairs inside the complex. Whoa! After a couple of steps I became very light-headed and had to stop. There is not much air here—there is definitely a lack of that oxygen stuff. I remember from high school that over half of the earth's atmospheric mass is below 10,000 feet. I can now personally attest that this appears to be correct.

We had lunch at a small cafeteria inside the complex. And afterwards, we took a small elevator up to the highest point of the complex known as the Sphinx. Here you could, if you were so inclined, go out onto an observation deck. We did. It was really cold, particularly with the wind. But what a view. It is indeed the top of Europe.

To the north is a huge glacier. It winds through a valley and to the west of the Eiger. You might remember the Clint Eastwood movie *The Eiger Sanction*, about a climb of the Eiger's north face. Whether you do or not, this is it.

We started our journey back down at 1:30 and arrived back in Grindelwald at four o'clock. As you might imagine, the ride down though the alpine valleys and meadows with the dappled afternoon sun peeking through the clouds was spectacular. It is interesting that all the houses in the valley below us are of the same style and face the same direction. Could be because of the wind and snow.

In Grindelwald it was good to have more air.

Ouch

"Oww!"

This is not a good thing to hear from your wife, regardless of whether or not you are in a foreign country. She was in the shower. The soap dispenser fell off the wall and broke her toe. Not an auspicious way to start the day.

I straightened it out and taped it to her other toes. There is not a lot you can do for broken toes. In theory, there was not going to be a lot of walking on this day as we were traveling to Lausanne by train so we'd be fine. The hotel proprietor gave us a ride to the station.

When we got to the Grindelwald station, there was a train for Interlaken fixing to leave, and if we had not had luggage and one of us hobbling, we might have tried to make it. We let it go. Besides, we had ticket issues to attend to.

We caught the next train to Interlaken. And, with Shirley not moving too quickly, it was good that our car, 1st class, was the first car at the station. We had it to ourselves, a good thing. Because we had the car to ourselves, we could put the windows down and I could bounce from side to side. I was like a dog in a car that can't decide which side of the car he wants to hang out of.

The trip to Interlaken takes about 40 minutes and has three or four 30-second stops. We got to Interlaken in plenty of time to make our next train, the *Golden Panorama*, through the Alps.

Our train arrived and we found our assigned car, #11, and our assigned seats. I mention this because you often don't have assigned seats, even in 1st class. Our ticket said we were traveling from Interlaken Ost (east) to Montreux. From Montreux we were to take a separate train to Lausanne on Lake Geneva.

I noted, however, that our ticket read, "*via Spiez*Zweisimmen*". I suspected that this meant we had to change trains somewhere. I asked a conductor and this indeed was what it meant; we had to change trains in Zweisimmen.

From Interlaken to Zweisimmen we were indeed in a panorama car. It had really big windows and the scenery was spectacular. It took us over an hour to get to Zweisimmen.

When we got to Zweisimmen more of a connection point than a station, we saw that there was indeed another train that read, "to Montreux." We had a small problem. There were cars #10 and #12, but no #11. Hmm. We got on because when changing trains in Switzerland, you don't have a lot of time. You don't dawdle.

Is This Where We Are Supposed To Be?

Not long after we left Zweisimmen, a conductor came along and showing her our tickets we asked, "Is this were we are supposed to be?" Answer: "No. Car #11 is at the front of the train." *This makes perfect sense.* The conductor said we could change cars in Gstad.

At the stop prior to Gstad, the conductor came to us and said, "Change cars now!" Easier said than done. Particularly with me handling most of the luggage and Shirley limping. The not much walking idea we had had earlier was out the window and we'd thought this was going to be an easy day for Shirley's foot. The conductor lady actually helped us (pulling Shirley's luggage) to get us to car #11. It was quite a ways and we barely made it.

Ok, now we are in car #11 and headed to Montreux. The conductor helped us stash our luggage by the door and proceeded to take us to our seats. I don't know whether or not these were our assigned seats or not, but we were ushered to the front of the train. To the very front, the first row. It had a big windshield facing forward and we were placed dead center. We would be the first people on the train to arrive in Montreux. Cool. We could not have had a better view. I believe the train driver was above us. It was a bit like being on a rollercoaster.

13. Brussels & the Netherlands

Brussels in Belgium is an easy place to visit. There is a lot to do and see, getting into town is easy, and the food is good.

Moules & Frites

I fell asleep just as the plane took off on our 45-minute flight to Brussels (also known as Bruxelles) from London. I was beat; we had flown in from the US into Heathrow and now on into Belgium.

Because we were both tired and not thinking too fast it was a good thing that our arrival and processing through passport control in Brussels was a piece of cake. While waiting for our luggage I got some Euros from a nearby cash machine and then more good news, our luggage showed up.

Getting into Brussels from the airport was also a piece of cake. Below the terminal is a train station that takes you right into town. It was not as far as I thought. One should be aware that European cities have, as I've noted several times, multiple train stations, and Brussels is no exception. It's a good idea to know which one you want. My reconnoitering before we arrived in Brussels told us that we wanted the *Gare du Nord*, the north train station. From here we could and did take a taxi to our hotel. In reality, the Central Station would have been closer. In any case, we made it to our hotel, the *Dominican.*

Shirley found the *Dominican* on the web and thought it looked nice, and it was reasonably priced. She also thought it would be a good location and she was right. Even though the hotel is in an older building, it is somewhat contemporary. To me, in Europe, contemporary means, among other things, strange bathroom fixtures—sometimes not as functional as you'd like. European hotels also often have strange elevators. We visited three floors before we could get the elevator doors to open on ours.

By now it was dinnertime. Now, Brussels is known for its seafood and, according to Shirley's guidebook, a good restaurant, *Chez Leon,* was very close to our hotel. As it turned out, the street (lane would be a better description) that we wanted, where a number of the popular restaurants are located, was only a half block away. A good thing.

We had *moules* and *frites* (mussels and fries). They are very popular here, as they are in Paris. They come in a variety of styles or preparations. Shirley had the Provencal style and I had the Escargot style. Really, really good. Assuming you like mussels. Speaking of mussels, the last time we were in Paris, they did not seem as popular as they once were. Times change.

Even though we had been awake for days, or so it seemed, we walked a block or so to a central square, the *Grote Markt* or Grand Place, where the Belgian equivalent to the *La Passeggiata,* the evening stroll, was in full swing. After one lap around the square, we headed back to our hotel and much needed sleep.

Chocolate and Bruegels

We slept like rocks. While I can't say we awoke feeling refreshed, we were a great deal better than the night before.

We set out fairly early is search of a particular pastry/coffee shop that Shirley had read about. She does a lot of research. I was just looking for some European coffee. Alas, we could not find the shop. We ended up back at the *Grote Markt,* where we found a place that had a sign out indicating they had breakfast. We sat at a table outside where I got my coffee.

We were on a square, we were in Europe, it was a Saturday, so there was a wedding. To us it seemed a bit early, but perhaps not so to them. City Hall is on the square, so this is where the wedding was to take place. Watching the *show* was our breakfast entertainment.

The morning was glorious. We had blue skies and a cool temperature. On the square, there were photo opportunities everywhere, from architectural wonders to statues both at ground level and high up on pinnacles.

During breakfast we discussed our plans for the day. Option one was to explore Brussels, and option two was to take the train to Bruges, a much smaller, and some say more picturesque city. Alas, we could not do both because the next day we were to take the train to Amsterdam to catch a cruise on the Rhine. We decided on Brussels. It was easier.

In Brussels, one of the things tourists seem to have a great need to do is see the *Manneken Pis*, the statue of a small naked boy peeing. It wasn't far, just down the *Rue de l'Etuve*.

According to legend (found on Wikipedia), during the 14th century, Brussels was under siege by a foreign power. The city had held its ground for some time, so the attackers conceived of a plan to place explosive charges at the city walls. A little boy named Julianske happened to be spying on them as they were preparing. He urinated on the burning fuse and thus saved the city.[3] Is this TMI, too much information, or is it history? Hmm.

While the statue is not even two feet high, it is enormously popular. So much so that people from all over the world send costumes for him. The day we saw him, he was dressed in green pants and a red sports coat with some sort of emblem on it. It meant nothing to us.

What did mean something to us were the incredible pastries in the shop windows lining the narrow street. Most everyone knows that Brussels is known for its chocolates. Well, it is also known for its pastries. We had to try some. Shirley thought the chocolates were so-so, but the pastry was very good. Yum.

---

[3] http://en.wikipedia.org/wiki/Manneken_Pis

Brussels, like London and many other European cites, has a hop-on, hop-off bus. They are usually two-level buses with the top open and are a really good way to see the city. They also usually come with headsets that tell you what you are seeing—in several languages. We hopped-on and chose English.

One of the places we hopped off was the Royal Museum of Fine Arts, on *Regentschapsstraat*. I won't go into too much detail about the museum except to say that it has two parts, the Ancient Art Museum with art from the 15th—17th centuries, and the Modern Art Museum with art of the 19th and 20th centuries. A lot of the ancient art was *really* odd, in particular paintings by Pieter Bruegel and Hans Memling. There was one painting in particular that looked to have Frankenstein's monster as the main character—he was green and looked to be *slightly* dead. In another painting all the people had the same face. Either they were all from the same family or the artist could only afford one model. There were a lot of unattractive people in these pictures.

The museum had a nice little café where we grabbed some lunch, a quiche and ham sandwich. There was a loggia outside where we sat to eat overlooking the rooftops of Brussels.

With regard to the language in Belgium, it is mostly French. Belgium is essentially a bilingual country, mostly French and Dutch or Flemish. In Brussels, it is more French, in Bruges, where we considered going, it's more

Dutch—it's closer to The Netherlands. We used French whenever we could (what little we know).

After lunch we hopped back on the hop-on, hop-off bus and sat up top for a tour of the city. Along the way we got a Belgian history lesson from a voice in our headsets. Kids in the US have it easy. We've only had presidents and our history is only 400 years or so. Belgium goes back a great deal further and has had so many changes in government in the past 1,000 years it is enough to make your head spin.

The Bizarre

We got off the bus near the train station and headed back towards the *Grote Markt*. As we got closer we could not believe all the people. As it turned out there was a parade—I use the term loosely—a parade that could possibly be called *Parade of the Bizarre*. It was actually the *Zinneke* Parade. It is a biennial parade that has a different theme each time. Costumes are very colorful, imaginative and often a bit bizarre. The closest thing I could compare it to would be a themed Mardi Gras parade or the Sambadrome in Rio de Janeiro, only on a smaller scale and without the floats and beads, and with more clothes. We merged right in with the participants and were swallowed up in the reveries.

We stepped out of the parade when we passed the *Galerie de la Reine*, a concourse that was a shopping mall of sorts. Fascinating window displays and lots of chocolate shops. Lots of chocolate shops. Hooray for Belgian Chocolate.

Mrs. C. had plans for dinner. As expected. In other words, she had a couple of specific restaurants in mind. As is often the case, we did not find them so we just plopped ourselves down at a table at the *Bistro Bourgeois* on the *Rue des Bouchers*. It was an excellent dinner that included paella and scallops, ostensibly *Coquille St. Jacques*. Generally, *Coquille St. Jacques* does not have a tomato and basil sauce. This did, nonetheless it was good.

At dinner, a couple of Americans sat down at the table next to us. We presumed a father and his son. The younger man was taking lots of food pictures. It turned out that he was a professional food photographer. He shot for *Bon Appetite* and *Food and Wine*, among others. While there is no particular anecdote to this story, I have frequently have found it both interesting and informative to talk to fellow English speaking patrons when dining out in other part of the world. You often get great suggestions.

Another slight digression: We were having dinner in restaurant in Lisbon not long after 9/11 when we struck up a conversation with a couple of local gentlemen at a nearby by table. They had questions for us since it was obvious to them that we were American. What was going to happen to New York? Was the World Trade Center going to be rebuilt. Their opinion, "It must be rebuilt! In Europe, we would rebuild." People are fascinating.

Amsterdam Cold Conundrum

It is fun to shop in the Amsterdam markets regardless of whether or not you buy anything. At the flower markets, there was nothing we could bring back to the US due to customs regulations; we knew we should not attempt entry into the US with plants, flowers or bulbs. We definitely could not bring back things from the head shops that sold marijuana and drug-related implements. In Amsterdam, "coffee shops" sell marijuana and "caffes" (Dutch spelling) sell coffee. It can be confusing. It is interesting that with all the tolerance for drugs (and sex), you cannot go into a pharmacy and buy cold capsules. You can get high, but you can't clear your head when you have a cold or allergies. This is true even for cold medications that don't contain things you can turn into narcotics. It is odd, indeed. And, annoying. It is the Amsterdam Cold Conundrum.

Are We Sinking?

Heading north on the English Channel on a cruise, we needed to get from the North Sea to Amsterdam where we were to disembark. You would think you would need to go around the Dutch peninsula and then head south. Fortunately, there is a shortcut called the Noordzeekanaal or the North Sea Canal. It is a ship canal between Amsterdam and the North Sea built between 1865 and 1876. We would transit this canal and its locks around one a.m.

Around 2:15 a.m. I awoke to gurgling noises. Naturally, I thought I should investigate. In our bathroom, I found the tub full of light brown water with large clumps of brown stuff (not sewage, more likely algae from the pipes). Both the tub and the sink were making gurgling noises. Odd. I made sure that the tub drain was fully opened and the water went down a bit, but not much. I called the front desk. At this time of night, the call went to the ship's bridge. I told them there was some sort of problem and described it to them. They said they'd send someone. I figured Mrs. C. and I should get dressed.

The someone who came was a ship maintenance person. He opened a wall panel above the toilet, did something, and the water started to drain. He said that the problem was the result of draining the ship's small pool, two decks above us. This seemed a strange explanation. The good news was that we were not sinking.

Ten minutes later the tub was full again. I called again, and this time two people came. The tub must have overflowed because the rug in front of the tub was wet. Again they got it drained, but the carpet outside the bathroom door was now quite wet. I did not think the water that wet our cabin floor had come from the tub; the bathroom floor was not wet.

I went out into the hall and saw the luggage to be collected when we reached Amsterdam was still there and that the carpet was wet in front of the doors of the two cabins next to us, aft. This was really not a good sign. I believe this is where the water in our cabin came from. The people in the adjoining cabins were not yet awake and had not discovered the problem.

Neither of us ever really got back to sleep.

I will shorten this story by saying that we talked to the ship's hotel manager, and he told us that the cruise line would give us a refund of some sort. Fine by us. He also told us that the real problem was going to be getting all this cleaned up before the next set of passengers arrived in about eight hours. This was a situation where we could have used a red button. Alas, there was no red button to push.

In Closing

It is my sincere wish that you have enjoyed the experiences I have related here, and that one or two of them brought a smile to your face. Whether you are an experienced traveler or just starting out exploring the world, I hope you have seen here that often *going with the flow* and/or just being observant can make a world of a difference whether your adventure is good or bad. Either way it is still an adventure.

I hope to share more with you in the future. . .

Epilogue

There is a framed quote on my desk that reads: *I am not the same having seen the moon shine on the other side of the world.* It is true. I keep this in mind when I travel.

Sometimes the goal of travel is to see things, and do things that are outside your comfort zone, outside the familiar. This can lead to things that can change your life, or at a minimum give you an experience that you remember your entire life. Sometimes, the seemingly mundane can become a memorable life experiences.

I will leave you with two quotes. The first was given to me by the hotel manager on a riverboat.

The world is a book, and those who do not travel read only a page.
—St. Augustine

The second, I hope you have heard before.

Life is not measured by the number of breaths we take, but by the moments that take our breath away."
—Hilary Cooper

Acknowledgements

As with any book, it takes a number of people to make it happen. I would like to express my gratitude to each of them.

First and foremost I must thank my wife Shirley for giving me the support and encouragement to produce this work.

Second, I must acknowledge that in a few of the stories the Mrs. C. mentioned was my first wife, Barbara. These are *Getting Started*, *In the Beginning*, *Easy Walk*, *CIGSMARBASIN*, and *Buckets of Water*.

I also must acknowledge the encouragements, style observations and general thoughts given to me by Sally Mayo, my alpha reader. Thank you.

Yet another individual who provided guidance was Dave Bly, a dear, dear friend and fellow author. It was Dave who introduced me to editor Matt Simon. It was Matt who guided me through antecedents, personal pronouns and such, making revisions without losing the gist and tone of the story.

Finally, I would like to thank Karimah Dossa, our fabulous travel agent who helped with planning many of the trips mentioned herein.

About the Author

Originally from South Florida, Van Chesnutt now lives in the Pacific Northwest, where he works as a computing consultant. He has travelled much of the United States, Europe, the South Pacific, and parts of Australia.